The Beaux-Arts Medal in America

Barbara A. Baxter

New York City

September 26, 1987, to April 16, 1988

The American Numismatic Society

ISBN 0-89722-221-0

Cover: Proof cast of the
Award Medal for the World's
Columbian Exposition, Chicago,
1893, by Augustus Saint-Gaudens,
catalogue number ***86***.

Printed by Braun-Brumfield, Inc., Ann Arbor

Table of Contents

Preface

"The making of medals has, through the reducing machine, gradually during the past fifty years changed from an art apart to a branch of sculpture. They now can be produced by any sculptor who has a sentiment of relief. Although I am not very old, I can remember the time when there were practically no medalists in this country, certainly no artists who made medals." In these words from his 1921 address accepting the American Numismatic Society's Saltus Medal for achievement in medallic art, John Flanagan summed up an extraordinarily fertile period for an artistic medium which, at least in America, had earlier been viewed chiefly as a carrier of messages.

In its earliest phase, in the fifteenth and sixteenth century, the medal was a small cast sculpture, distinctive in its form and iconography, within the technical capabilities of any sculptor. It was a medium employed by painters such as Pisanello, sculptors such as Leone Leoni, and carvers such as Peter Flötner. With the ascendency of the struck medal in the seventeenth century, medal making required proficiency in die engraving, a skill developed chiefly by gem cutters and, especially, coin makers. It was only with the development in the nineteenth century of the Janvier lathe, which transferred modeled reliefs into dies, that sculptors could again include medals among their works.

Parallel to the concentration of medallic art in the hands of coin makers has been a concentration of its collection and study among numismatists. The American Numismatic Society has by far the largest holdings of American medals of the Beaux-Arts period, and the standard reference in this area has been the catalogue of its 1910 International Exhibition of Contemporary Medals. In recent years, as interest has increased in the work of American sculptors of the Beaux-Arts tradition, their medals have been considered in the context of their entire oeuvre and have been included in exhibitions and catalogues often devoted to the work of a single artist.

The goal of this exhibition is to situate the American Beaux-Arts medal in its historical and artistic context. To this end we have been very fortunate to have secured the services of Barbara A. Baxter as Guest Curator for the exhibition. Ms Baxter, whose background includes strong qualifications in numismatics and art history, has taken full responsibility for the organization of the exhibit. She has selected material from our extensive holdings and has surveyed public and private collections for loan material. She has written the catalogue entries and the interpretive essays in this catalogue and has supervised the design and mounting of the exhibition. This exhibit would not have been possible without her sure judgement and untiring dedication.

Colleagues from many institutions have been most generous in sharing with us information on their holdings and arranging loans for this show. The Council, the Committee on Medals, and the staff of the American Numismatic Society have been a consistent source of encouragement and assistance. A loyal group of patrons has provided financial as well as moral support for the mounting of the exhibition and the publication of the catalogue. We record here our sincere gratitude to John W. Adams; the American Medallic Sculpture Association; the American Numismatic Association; Janis Conner and Joel Rosenkranz; Harry W. Fowler; the Sharon R. and David L. Ganz Endowment; Robert A. La Rocca; Malcolm & Hayes, Howard Wasserman, President; the Metropolitan New York Numismatic Convention; R. Henry Norweb; Presidential Coin and Antique Co., H. Joseph Levine, President; Mrs. Marion Russell, Stephen K. Scher; and Erich Wronker.

Alan M. Stahl
Curator of Medals
American Numismatic Society

Acknowledgements

The initial idea for this exhibition was proposed by Alan Stahl, Curator of Medieval Coins and of Medals at the ANS. The biennial congress of the Federation Internationale de la Médaille, which will be held in the United States for the first time this September, provided the occasion for the mounting of this exhibition of medallic sculpture from the period of the medium's greatest flourishing in America. "The Beaux-Arts Medal in America" is designed to offer an historical complement to the major exhibit of contemporary medals which will be shown at the FIDEM Congress in Colorado.

In the course of organizing this exhibition, I have been greatly assisted by a number of museum colleagues and private collectors, who have generously shared their knowledge and responded to my requests for loans. I would like especially to thank Lauretta Dimmick, Museum of Fine Arts, Boston; Cynthia Kennedy Sam, Cambridge, Massachusetts; Suzanne Wallace, Saint-Gaudens National Historic Site, Cornish, New Hampshire; Dorothy Budd Bartle, The Newark Museum, Newark, New Jersey; Lewis Sharp and Donna Hassler, The Metropolitan Museum of Art, New York; Scott Miller, New York; Conner-Rosenkranz Galleries, New York; Nancy Johnson, American Academy and Institute of Arts and Letters, New York; George Gurney, National Museum of American Art, Smithsonian Institution, Washington, D.C.; and Cory Gillilland, National Numismatic Collection, Museum of American History, Smithsonian Institution, Washington, D.C. Donna Hassler, Scott Miller, and Cynthia Kennedy Sam kindly read and made helpful suggestions on sections of the catalogue text.

I also wish to gratefully acknowledge the assistance provided by my colleagues at the ANS. This project would not have been possible without the support of Director Leslie Elam. William Bischoff, Assistant Curator of Modern Coins, and Curator Alan Stahl contributed insightful essays to this catalogue. ANS Photographer Frank Deak and Darkroom Technician Charles Badal produced the excellent photographs for the catalogue. George Cuhaj has loaned a colorful souvenir postcard from the 1909 Hudson-Fulton Celebration for the exhibition, and Lori Rubens has provided technical assistance with the mounting of the exhibit. Alan Stahl and Marie Martin deserve special thanks for their careful editing of my manuscript. Marie is responsible for the thoughtful, creative design of the catalogue. Alan has guided my work with unflagging enthusiasm and good humor.

A particular debt of gratitude is owed the Department of American Paintings and Sculpture of the Metropolitan Museum of Art for their loan of the reduced-scale version of the Victory figure from Augustus Saint-Gaudens' Sherman Monument. We could not have found a more fitting centerpiece for this exhibition than the work which inspired Saint-Gaudens' beautiful design for the U.S. twenty-dollar gold piece, the epitome of the artistic quality and elegance of the Beaux-Arts medal in America.

Finally, I would like to thank my husband Marc Postman and my sister Nancy Baxter for the personal support which they have given me while I was working on this project.

Barbara A. Baxter
Guest Curator

Introduction

In the decades between 1880 and the First World War, the art of the medal experienced a remarkable flowering in America. Neither before nor since that time has medallic sculpture enjoyed such popularity in this country. With its emphasis on the glorification of public events and private achievements, the medal was an especially powerful art form for transmitting the self-image of turn-of-the-century America. The barons of industry, the great Expositions celebrating technology and progress, the politicians, the artists, and the socialites of the "Gilded Age" are all chronicled by the medals of the period.

Before the 1880s, the production of medals in this country had been in the hands of a few specialists trained in engraving and die cutting. With advances in the technology of the reducing machine, however, the medium became accessible to any artist schooled in modeling, liberating medallic art from its strictly commemorative function and allowing it to develop as a branch of sculpture. For the first time professional sculptors assumed a leading role in the designing of medals, and almost every major American sculptor of the Beaux-Arts era created medals or medallic portraits. While the term "Beaux-Arts," commonly used to describe the style of sculpture produced in America between the 1876 Centennial Exposition and World War I, is a somewhat unsatisfactory label for a considerable range of individual styles, it broadly defines certain general features of the sculpture of this period: "an academic emphasis on the human form," a reliance on classical, Renaissance and Baroque models, and a technical facility learned in France.[1]

Above all, the shift from Rome, the source of the neoclassical style which had prevailed in American sculpture in the decades before the Civil War, to Paris, the new center for training in sculpture, was central to the flourishing of sculptural and medallic art in late nineteenth-century America. Earlier in the century, French sculpture had undergone a revolution in style and technique. A new manner of lively rich modeling suitable to casting in bronze replaced the smoothly carved marble surfaces of neoclassical sculpture. The growing desire of American sculptors to work in bronze led them to seek the instruction in modeling offered by the Paris art schools. The Petite Ecole (renamed the Ecole des Arts Décoratifs in 1877), the Ecole des Beaux-Arts, and the private art academies of Paris provided them with a systematic education in sculptural technique. After completing preliminary courses in drawing and modeling at one of the other art schools, many of the Americans were accepted to the Ecole des Beaux-Arts, where they worked primarily in the ateliers of François Jouffroy and his younger followers, Jean Falguière and Antonin Mercié, all exponents of a naturalistic style of academic bronze sculpture.[2]

The revolution in modeled sculpture, initiated by the great sculptor David d'Angers, spawned a "Renaissance of the medal" in France, which also commenced with David.[3] In his extraordinary series of portrait medallions, begun in 1827, David revived the cast technique of Italian Renaissance medals, rescuing the art of the medal from the banality to which it had descended in the hands of neoclassical engravers. His boldly modeled, intensely Romantic medallic portraits have the immediacy of sketches, but they are in fact carefully studied. Following David's example, virtually every French

Fig. 1
296

Fig. 2
3

sculptor after 1830 produced portrait medallions as a supplement to the normal range of sculptural commissions. By the 1850s, medals were no longer exhibited with prints and engravings at the Paris Salons, as they had been earlier in the century, but were included in the sculpture section.[4] The advent of the reducing machine in the 1830s facilitated this development. The reducing machine, which is depicted on a medal created by J. Edouard Roiné for the Joseph K. Davison firm of Philadelphia (fig. 1, ***296***), gave sculptors the freedom to model the design for a medal or portrait medallion on a large scale and then have it mechanically reduced.[5] For struck pieces, a specialized machine was used to engrave a reduced copy of the model directly into a steel die, eliminating the need for laborious hand cutting of dies.[6]

Fig. 3
9

An important figure in the French revival of medallic art, who also played a key role in inspiring the American Beaux-Arts sculptors to model portrait medallions, was Henri Chapu. In his cast portrait medallions, patterned after the work of David, Chapu developed a new style of refined, low relief modeling (fig. 2, ***3***), which Louis Oscar Roty later credited with affecting the entire subsequent "evolution of glyptic art" in France.[7] Chapu trained many pupils in this style of modeling at the Académie Julian, where John Flanagan, Hermon MacNeil and Bela Pratt, among other Americans, studied with him.

While the acknowledged leaders of the late nineteenth-century renaissance of the medal in France, Jules-Clément Chaplain and Louis Oscar Roty, did not influence the course of American medallic art as strongly as did Chapu, they were instrumental in popularizing the art of the medal in Europe and abroad. Chaplain, whom Mark Jones has called "the first great artist to make use of the flexibility offered by the reducing machine," demonstrated, with his masterful portrait medallions, "that a single model, properly conceived, could be successful both as a cast plaque on a large scale and as a struck medal or plaquette on a small scale."[8] The version of Chaplain's beautifully modeled portrait of Madame Jeanne Mathilde Claude illustrated here (fig. 3, ***9***) is a bronze cast from his original model for the piece, which was also issued as a smaller cast medal. In contrast to the sober draftsmanship of Chaplain's medals, the works of his pupil Roty feature a more delicate, painterly approach to low relief modeling, derived from Chapu. Roty's revival of the rectangular plaquette format, which had not been used since the Renaissance, allowed him to give the medal a more frankly pictorial treatment. His lyrical, allegorial figure-compositions and soft-edged style were imitated by a host of medalists in France and elsewhere in Europe, and the sand-blasting process which he employed to give his medals an even softer tone became standard practice in the production of medals.[9]

Olin Levi Warner and Augustus Saint-Gaudens, the first of the American Beaux-Arts sculptors to take up medallic portraiture, arrived in Paris in the late 1860s, and in 1870 both worked in Jouffroy's atelier at the Ecole des Beaux-Arts.[10] Warner began making portrait medallions before Saint-Gaudens, exhibiting a "colossal medallion" in plaster of the actor Edwin Forrest at the 1876 Philadelphia Centennial Exhibition. Charles de Kay's later criticism of this piece for its "peculiar broadness and boldness in relief" and "almost brutal" effect explains why Warner's vigorously modeled portrait medallions did not achieve the immediate success of Saint-Gaudens' more refined portrait reliefs.[11] Warner's striking medallic portraits of the 1870s and '80s (**68** and **69**, for example), which recall the works of David d'Angers and Chapu in format and modeling technique, deserve greater recognition than they have received both for their artistic quality and for their position as the earliest works of medallic art in this country to reflect the resurgence of the cast medal in France.

Saint-Gaudens' tremendously successful portrait reliefs, which he referred to as "medallions" despite their generally rectangular format, created a taste for portrait plaques and medallions among the nation's elite. In Rome, where he went after Paris, Saint-Gaudens fell under the spell of the early Renaissance sculptors Pisanello and Donatello, and he brought with him casts of their bas-reliefs when he returned to New York in 1875. Although his friend the painter John LaFarge encouraged him at that time to model in low relief in emulation of the fifteenth-century masters, it was not until he returned to Paris in 1877 that Saint-Gaudens, "upon seeing the portrait of 'A Man with a Hat' by the French sculptor, Chapu...promptly set out to model bas-reliefs of the group of artists about him...."[12] In the remarkable series of portrait reliefs which he created in the late 1870s and early 1880s (**73** and ***74***, for example), Saint-Gaudens developed a new style of exquisite low relief modeling, notable for its lively, irregular surfaces. With only the slightest variation in the relief, the sculptor was able to produce a bravura effect, manipulating the play of light and shade across the surface of the bronze in an "impressionistic" manner.[13] His reliefs are also unique for the way in which he incorporated the portrait into a larger design, devoting as much attention to the background, molding, lettering and other decorative details as to the subject.

Saint-Gaudens' medals, like his portrait reliefs, had a great impact on the progress of American

Fig. 4
77

medallic art. His first and most important official medal is the piece which he designed for the New York celebration of the centennial of George Washington's inauguration in 1889 (fig. 4, *77*). The sculptor's elegant design for the obverse of this medal, based on a composition frequently employed by Pisanello, the greatest of the Italian Renaissance medalists, established a format that would be repeatedly exploited by his followers and their students for two generations to come.[14] In technique, as well as in format and lettering, Saint-Gaudens' Washington medal, which Victor Brenner later singled out as a notable "stepping stone toward the development of our modern [American] medallic art," is faithful to its Quattrocento sources.[15] Significantly, the piece was cast, in the Renaissance tradition, preserving the lively texture of the relief.

After the French academic tradition, the Renaissance models introduced by Saint-Gaudens provided the second important source of inspiration for the flowering of medallic art in America. While the French nineteenth-century medalists looked to the Quattrocento for only general inspiration, their American contemporaries were more literal in their following of Renaissance prototypes. This reliance on fifteenth-century artistic sources was one aspect of a growing tendency among Americans in the 1880s and 1890s to identify with the period of the Italian Renaissance.[16] An art form which had been developed in the fifteenth century to glorify the individual was uniquely suited to the portrayal of America's new "merchant princes." As artist and critic Kenyon Cox wrote in an 1887 article extolling Saint-Gaudens and his revival of bas-relief sculpture: "There only [in the sculpture of the Renaissance] could they [Saint-Gaudens and his contemporaries] find the modern man with his pronounced individuality and his special development of character, and there only could they find the means of representing him in their art."[17]

The professionalization of American sculpture in this period also helped to encourage the patronage of medallic sculpture. The Constitution of the National Sculpture Society, founded in May 1893 by Saint-Gaudens and his Paris trained colleagues as "the American center for the promulgation of the Beaux-Arts style," stated that one of the goals of the organization was to "foster the taste for, and encourage the production of, ideal sculpture for the household."[18] The reproductions of Saint-Gaudens' portrait reliefs furnished a model for the successful marketing of small-scale sculpture. For both commercial and aesthetic reasons, he continually reworked his most popular pieces to create a series of limited editions.[19]

The spectacular Expositions and Celebrations of the "American Renaissance," which showcased the Beaux-Arts style in their grandiose programs of decorative sculpture, provided a unique occasion for the production of huge numbers of commemorative medals and tokens.[20] America's foremost medallic sculptors were commissioned to design the official medals for the World's Fairs of 1893, 1901, 1904, and 1915, as well as the New York Hudson-Fulton Celebration of 1909. Saint-Gaudens once more set the precedent with his award medal for the 1893 World's Columbian Exposition (cover, ***86***, and ***87***). The naturalism and vitality of his pictorial composition for the obverse of this piece, again reminiscent of Renaissance relief sculpture, are in marked contrast to the more decorative, academic style of the medals created by European artists for the Exposition.

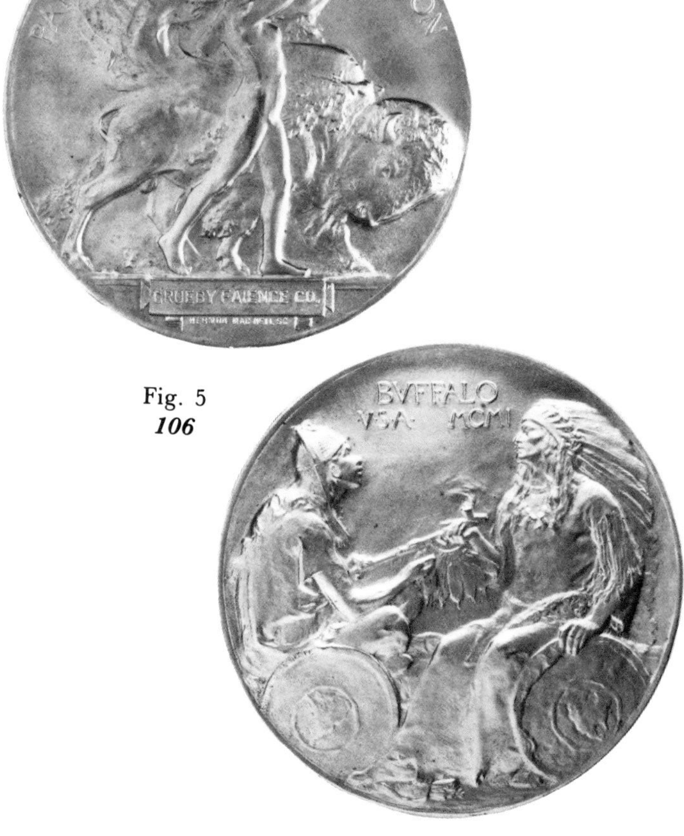

Fig. 5
106

Fig. 6
191

The Columbian Exposition and the World's Fairs that followed it stimulated American artists to develop a distinctively American subject matter in order to represent "the pageant of their country." Hermon MacNeil's award medal for the 1901 Pan-American Exposition is indicative of this trend (fig. 5, ***106***). MacNeil himself said of this piece that he aimed "to produce a design that could be mistaken for nothing not American."[21] Fascinated by the Indians whom he had met in the sideshows at the Columbian Exposition, MacNeil traveled to the Southwest to visit their reservations, and his firsthand observation of native Americans is evident in his unidealized treatment of the Indian figures on the reverse of the Pan-American Exposition medal. The imagery of the buffalo and the Indian which MacNeil employed for this medal, as well as his naturalistic style, anticipate James Earle Fraser's 1913 "buffalo" nickel (***194***), the first U.S. coin to make use of this type of American symbolism.

Truly international in scope, the World's Expositions catered to a new cosmopolitan spirit in turn-of-the-century America. At the Expositions, the American public had a chance to view the latest in European art, including medallic art, and as a result the demand for things European in this country increased. American patrons commissioned medals from European artists, most notably Roty and the Austrian medalist Scharff, who worked in a similarly elegant manner.[22] Through George Lucas, an American art agent in Paris, the New York philanthropist and art dealer Samuel P. Avery assembled a substantial collection of the works of David d'Angers, Chaplain and Roty, which he presented to the Metropolitan Museum of Art in 1897. An active member of the American Numismatic Society and advocate of medallic art, Avery also took an interest in the career of Victor Brenner and gave the young medalist a letter of introduction to Lucas when he left for Paris in 1898. Through Lucas, Brenner obtained an introduction to Roty, with whom he subsequently studied and worked as an assistant.[23] Although Roty's medals were very popular in the United States, his work had little direct influence on the indigenous school of medalists, with the exception of Brenner, whose style bears the strong imprint of his mentor. Statements gathered from a number of prominent American sculptors by George Kunz for a tribute to the French medalist imply that while they admired Roty's work, the medals of the Renaissance held a greater attraction for them.[24]

At the same time that Brenner was in Paris, many other American sculptors were working and studying there. Frederick MacMonnies, a former assistant to Saint-Gaudens, and Janet Scudder, a pupil of MacMonnies, had established their own studios in Paris, and Saint-Gaudens was again working there in the late 1890s, employing a number of younger American sculptors as assistants in his studio.[25] Following the lead of Saint-Gaudens, many of these sculptors produced small portrait reliefs to supplement their income from other commissions. It had become fashionable for cosmopolitan Americans to sit for a portrait medallion in Paris, just as they posed for portraits by expatriate painter John Singer Sargent. Works by Scudder (fig. 6, ***191***) and John Flanagan (***143***), another former assistant to Saint-Gaudens who worked in Paris for twelve years, illustrate the elegant style of medallic portraiture crafted by American artists in Paris. Scudder's portrait plaquette of a Woman with a Japanese Fan is typical of her work in its exquisite detail and her incorporation of an elaborate decorative frame into the design of the piece. The medallic work of Saint-Gaudens, Flanagan, and Scudder received favorable notice from Leonce Benedite in his review of the medals exhibited at the Paris Salon of 1899.[26] In a survey of the medals exhibited a year later at the Universal Exposition in Paris, the French critic Roger Marx singled out the works by medalists from the United States, Austria and the Netherlands for their distinctive style and quality. All of the American artists who exhibited medals or portrait medallions at the 1900 Exposition, Saint-Gaudens, Brenner, Flanagan, and MacMonnies, receive special mention in Marx's essay.[27]

While American medallic art was winning praise abroad, appreciation for the medium was steadily increasing at home. The campaign to improve the artistic quality of the U.S. coinage, spearheaded by the American Numismatic Society and the National Sculpture Society, reinforced the growth of interest in medals.[28] Those who demanded the redesign of the coinage found in President Theodore Roosevelt a willing champion. Victor Brenner said of Roosevelt in 1910 that "His efforts to introduce a change in our coinage have done more towards popularizing the art of the medalist than has any previous movement."[29] In 1905 Roosevelt commissioned Saint-Gaudens to undertake new designs for the ten-dollar and twenty-dollar gold pieces, the first time that an artist outside of the U.S. Mint had been entrusted with the design of a regular issue of this country's coinage. The success of Saint-Gaudens' designs (***201***, ***202***, and ***203***), which Roosevelt had inspired with his suggestion that the sculptor try for a coinage in high relief modeled after the numismatic masterpieces of ancient Greece, ensured that the entire series of U.S. coins would be redesigned by the country's leading medallic sculptors. The most lasting of the new designs, also chosen by Roosevelt, was Brenner's Lincoln cent (***193***), the first regular issue of U.S. coinage to feature the image of a historical figure. It is to Roosevelt's credit that he recognized the merit of Brenner's superbly modeled portrait of Lincoln, which the medalist had originally created for a plaquette and medal commemorating the one-hundredth anniversary of the President's birth (**136** and fig. 7, ***137***).

Enthusiasm for the art of the medal was at its height in the period between 1900 and the First World War. In 1894, it had been reported in the *American Journal of Numismatics* that only two machines for reducing and cutting dies from a model existed in the United States, one at the Gorham Manufacturing Company in Providence, Rhode Island, and the other at the U.S. Mint. At Tiffany & Company in New York, dies for medals were still being cut by hand.[30] By 1905, several new medal manufacturing firms equipped with the Janvier lathe, the latest in die cutting machines, were in competition with Tiffany and Gorham. The most important of these firms for the production of art medals were Joseph K. Davison's Sons in Philadelphia and the Medallic Art Company in New York. When Henry Hering, Saint-Gaudens' assistant responsible for modeling the new gold coins, complained to Theodore Roosevelt in 1907 that the reducing machine in use at the U.S. Mint was hopelessly out of date, the President promptly had a Janvier machine brought from Paris and installed.[31]

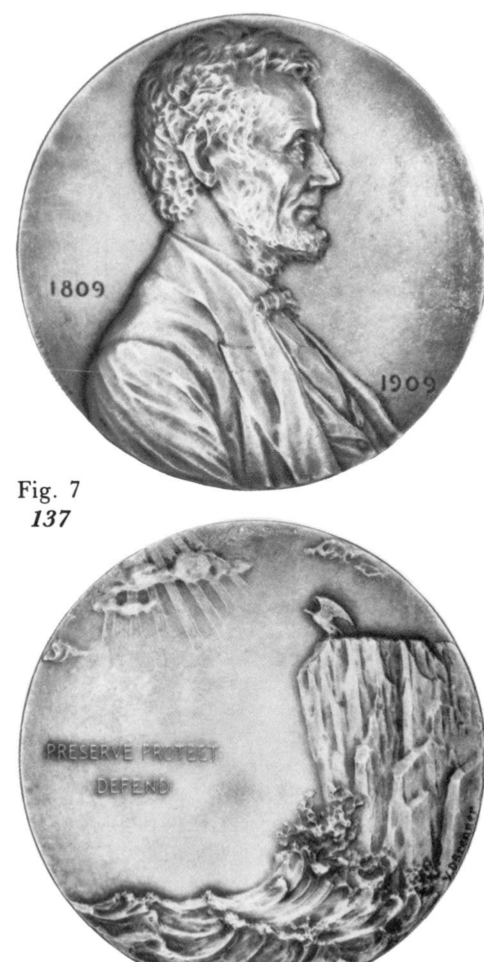

Fig. 7
137

The increase in facilities and improved technology for medal production supported a

Fig. 8
253

tremendous rise in demand for medals from individuals, businesses, and organizations. From 1905 through the First World War, the American Numismatic Society issued a series of medals of high artistic quality, commissioned from the foremost medalists and sculptors of the day, and the Society also lent its support to other organizations that wished to issue medals. Another society dedicated to the promotion of medallic art in America, the Circle of Friends of the Medallion, was formed in 1909. Patterned after similar groups in France, Austria and Belgium, the Circle of Friends already had about five hundred members in 1910.[32] In the six years of its existence the group issued a dozen medals, which were sold in unique book-shaped holders with an accompanying text on the artist and the subject of the piece. The majority of these medals feature softly modeled allegorical compositions in the continental style transmitted to this country by immigrant European artists.[33]

At the International Exhibition of Contemporary Medals presented by the American Numismatic Society in March 1910, the continental style of medallic art derived from Roty was very much in evidence, and exhibits by European medalists greatly outnumbered those by American artists.[34] In a review of the Exhibition, U.S. Mint Director A. Piatt Andrew commended its comprehensiveness and the wide range of subject matter and technique displayed. In his discussion of individual medalists, Andrew focused on the achievements of the French school, saying little about the Americans represented in the show.[35] The exhibit of works by Belgian medalist Godefroid Devreese, an exponent of the continental style, was judged the most successful by the Committee of Award for the Exhibition, and Devreese received the commission for a commemorative medal. The plaquette which he produced, with its bland allegorical compositions and fussy modeling, illustrates the weaknesses of the European academic tradition, and the piece was considered so unacceptable that only three examples of it were ever struck (fig. 8, *253*).

American medallic art flourished in the decade following the International Exhibition, and a list of the best medals ever produced in this country would comprise mainly works issued in those years. Significantly, it is not the works of immigrant medalists that would dominate such a list, but the medals by American artists trained in the Saint-Gaudens studio and the art schools of Paris. The importance of Saint-Gaudens as a mentor for younger American sculptors cannot be overestimated. Of the artists discussed in this catalogue, Philip Martiny, Frederick MacMonnies, Adolph A. Weinman, Bela Lyon Pratt, John Flanagan, James Earle Fraser, Helen Mears, Henry Hering and Francis Grimes all worked as assistants to the master sculptor.

Of the group of sculptors who worked with Saint-Gaudens, John Flanagan and James Earle Fraser were the most talented medalists. Cornelius Vermeule perceptively summarizes their

Fig. 10
152

Fig. 9
233

contribution to medallic art when he says that Flanagan and Fraser "achieved a perfect synthesis of the ideal, the real and the traditional in medallic design."[36] The works of both men stand out for their strong designs and skillful modeling. Fraser's medals are more closely indebted to Saint-Gaudens and to Renaissance sources than are Flanagan's, which are generally more original in composition and subject matter. Fraser's superb Harriman Memorial Medal for the American Museum of Safety (fig. 9, ***233***), issued in 1914, successfully blends "photographic naturalism" and Renaissance tradition. The obverse of this medal follows the Quattrocento format of Saint-Gaudens' George Washington medal (fig. 4, *77*), but Fraser's design is more tightly constructed and the portrait bust is given a more realistic treatment. The reverse of the Harriman medal is a masterpiece of medallic composition. The track walker who strides vigorously along the rails, as if ready to break free of the confines of the tondo, has a commanding presence, made tangible by Fraser's textured modeling.

Flanagan's medal for the Essex Agricultural Society of Massachusetts (fig. 10, ***152***) is much different in spirit from Fraser's Harriman. The two sides of the Essex medal depict opposing aspects of rural life. A scene of a mother and her children in the farmyard occupies the obverse of the medal, while the image of a man laboring with a shovel fills the reverse. Flanagan emphasizes the contrast between the idyllic, classicizing imagery of the obverse and the realistic subject matter of the reverse by executing the two sides of the piece in different styles. The obverse composition is modeled in a series of delicately rendered planes, whereas the powerful, muscular figure on the reverse rises boldly from the plain surface of the piece. In compositions such as the one created for the reverse of the Essex medal, Flanagan brought a new realism to medallic art.

Although World War I marked the end of the

Fig. 11
368

renaissance of the American medal, the entrance of the United States into the war provoked one last outburst of interest in medallic art. Medals and decorations were produced to honor deeds of bravery, recognize service, and commemorate specific events in the war. As Mark Jones has shown, the classical tradition of medallic art in France and America "allowed only the most inadequate of responses" to an ugly and cruel war.[37] While German medalists developed a new, expressionist idiom that enabled them to represent the brutality of the war, American artists continued to utilize the allegorical vocabulary of the continental tradition, or to work in a more naturalistic vein, tempered by idealism. Artistically one of the finest American war medals is the Mt. Sinai Hospital War Service Medal (fig. 12, ***328***) by Adolph A. Weinman, another of Saint-Gaudens' students. Weinman's classicizing style and his mastery of medallic design are apparent in this piece, which features an allegorical design based on Greco-Roman sources. The pathos of the wounded warrior, the heroic gesture of the woman who protects him, and the menacing demeanor of the German soldier are faithful to the classical tradition, but they create an impression almost of parody when considered in terms of the reality of the war.

A Victory medal for the Art War Relief created by Paul Manship (fig. 11, ***368***) illustrates the new mode of sculpture that came into favor in the early 1920s, supplanting the Beaux-Arts style. In Manship's work bold, linear stylizations replace the naturalistic modeling of the Saint-Gaudens school. The subject matter of this medal is, however, not at all new. The militant figure of Liberty, the American eagle and the rising sun are all familiar from the Beaux-Arts designs for U.S. coinage. Despite his radically different style, Manship was essentially conservative in retention of a classical, allegorical vocabulary. In the succeeding decades, neither the artists who followed Manship nor those who continued to work in the Beaux-Arts tradition would take American medallic art in significantly new directions.

Fig. 12
328

NOTES TO THE INTRODUCTION

1 Kathryn Greenthal, *Augustus Saint-Gaudens, Master Sculptor* (New York, 1985), p. 40. The best general works on American sculpture of this period are Lorado Taft's 1903 *History of American Sculpture*, revised by Adeline Adams in 1930, Wayne Craven's *Sculpture in America*, and the catalogue of the 1976 Whitney Museum exhibition *200 Years of American Sculpture*. A list of references and citation forms is included in the bibliography at the end of this volume.

2 For an analysis of the role of Paris in the development of American sculpture in this period, see Kathryn Greenthal, "Late Nineteenth Century American Sculpture in Its International Context," pp. 241-47 in *La Scultura nel XIX secolo*, Atti del XXIV Congresso internazionale di storia dell'arte, vol. 6 (Bologna, 1984). On the training offered by the Paris art schools, see Anne Wagner, "Learning to Sculpt in the Nineteenth Century," pp. 9-20 in *Romantics to Rodin* and see also pp. 28-31 in *La Sculpture française au XIXe siècle*, the catalogue of an exhibition at the Galéries Nationales du Grand Palais (Paris, 1986).

3 On the revival of the medal in France see the writings of Roger Marx listed in the general bibliography and a short article by the same author in English, "The Renaissance of the Medal in France," *The Studio* 15 (1899), pp. 14-22; also Jones, pp. 110-30, and below, pp. 15-22.

4 Jones, p. 110.

5 Numbers in bold type refer to catalogue entries; those in italics are illustrated.

6 The Roiné medal actually depicts both types of machines: the pantograph, used for reducing sculpture, and the Janvier lathe, a die cutting machine. If the sculptor's model, executed in a soft material such as wax or clay, was too large to fit on the lathe, it first had to be reduced on the pantograph. A replica of the model, produced by the electrotype process, was mounted on the lathe, and the machine then cut or engraved a reduced copy of the model in positive or negative into a softened steel die. After hand retouching, the metal was hardened, and the finished die was used for striking the medal. If the machine had produced a positive die, or "hub," as was most often the case, a negative die had to be made from it before striking. For a full discussion of the methods of medal making, see the pamphlet by Victor D. Brenner, *The Art of the Medal* (New York, 1910), reprinted in *The Numismatist* 95 (1982), pp. 2238-55, or Charles E. Barber's 1896 account of the process of die preparation reprinted in Julian, pp. xi-xlii.

7 Roty is quoted in Marx 1897, p. 12.

8 Jones, p. 120.

9 George F. Kunz, "The Late Louis Oscar Roty: His Life Work and His Influence on the Past and Future of Medallic Art," *AJN* 47 (1913), p. 106.

10 For Warner and Saint-Gaudens, see below, pp. 26-34.

11 Henry Eckford [Charles de Kay], "Olin Levi Warner, Sculptor," *The Century Magazine* 37 (1889), p. 393.

12 Homer Saint-Gaudens, ed., *The Reminiscences of Augustus Saint-Gaudens* (New York, 1913), vol. 1, pp. 215-16.

13 Greenthal 1985, p. 91.

14 Vermeule, p. 96.

15 Victor Brenner, "Brief Sketch of the Progress in the United States of Medallic Art," *Procès-Verbaux et mémoires du Congrès international de numismatique et d'art de la médaille contemporaine* (Brussels, 1910), p. 551 (article reprinted in *The Numismatist* 23 (1910), pp. 265-66).

16 The era was in fact already referred to in 1880 as the "American Renaissance." For general discussions of American art and culture in this period see *The American Renaissance, 1876-1917*, the catalogue of an exhibition at the Brooklyn Museum (Brooklyn, 1979) and Detroit 1983.

17 Kenyon Cox, "Augustus Saint-Gaudens," *The Century Magazine* 35 (1887), p. 30. In an earlier article Cox had discussed the achievement of the Quattrocento sculptors, since their work was "so great a factor in molding the art-thought" of his time: "Sculptors of the Early Italian Renaissance," *The Century Magazine* 29 (1884), pp. 62-66.

18 Craven, p. 419.

19 John Dryfhout has chronicled the many different versions of the Robert Louis Stevenson relief (***76***), the most popular of the editions of Saint-Gaudens' sculpture, in Jeanne L. Wasserman, ed., *Metamorphoses in Nineteenth-Century Sculpture* (Cambridge, MA, 1975), pp. 187-200.

20 See below, pp. 32-39.

21 The remark is quoted in *AJN* 36 (1901/2), p. 40.

22 For Scharff, see below, p. 67-68.

23 Lucas' diaries, which have been transcribed and published, provide a fascinating account of the

cosmopolitan art circles in Paris at the turn of the century. See Lillian C. Randall, ed., *The Diary of George A. Lucas: An American Art Agent in Paris, 1857-1909*, 2 vols. (Princeton, 1979). Brenner executed a portrait medallion of Lucas in 1899 (***119***), and both Brenner and Scharff produced medals in honor of Avery (**141** and **270**).

24 Kunz, pp. 107-8. Hermon MacNeil is quoted here as saying that Roty "as a medalist expressed very much the style that France has produced in sculpture during the last ten years. I mean that clean, fluent, aesthetic quality, that has considerable femininity in its makeup, as opposed to the more vigorously constructed medal of the Renaissance."

25 For MacMonnies and Scudder, see below, pp. 49-50, 56.

26 Leonce Benedite, "La Médaille au salon du 1899," *Art et Décoration* 6 (1899), p. 154.

27 Marx 1901, p. vii.

28 On the redesign of the coinage, see the essay by William Bischoff, below, pp. 51-53.

29 Brenner, "Brief Sketch," p. 552. On Roosevelt's support for the arts in general, see Glenn Brown, "Roosevelt and the Fine Arts," *The American Architect* 116 (1919), pp. 711-19, 737-52.

30 *AJN* 28 (1893/94), pp. 53-54, 79.

31 Henry Hering, "History of the $10 and $20 Gold Coins of 1907 Issue," *The Numismatist* 1949 (52), pp. 455-58. For Hering, see also p. 59 below.

32 Brenner, "Brief Sketch," p. 552.

33 For a discussion of the work of these immigrant medalists, see below, pp. 70-74.

34 On the International Exhibition, see below, pp. 65.

35 A. Piatt Andrew, "An International Medallic Exhibition," *The American Review of Reviews* 41 (1910), pp. 561-67, excerpted in *The Numismatist* 23 (1910), pp. 173-74.

36 Vermeule, p. 127. For Flanagan and Fraser, see below, pp. 43-46, 59-61.

37 Jones, p. 152. For the medals of World War I also see below, pp. 75-80.

Notes to the Catalogue

Each catalogue entry gives the following information: title of the work and date of issue, if known; issuing organization and/or purpose of the medal; artist (only in sections where works by more than one artist are catalogued); technique, metal, dimensions and firm responsible for production of the piece, if known; credit line; bibliographical references.

The terminology used here generally follows the 1911 ANS *Catalogue of the International Exhibition of Contemporary Medals* (IECM). In this catalogue, the term uniface denotes either a one-sided cast or a struck piece with a plain reverse. Any struck or cast piece not designated as uniface is understood to have both obverse and reverse designs. The term galvano refers to a uniface piece produced by the electrotype process, whereby a replica of the artist's model is created by electrodepositing a thin metal shell on the surface of the model or a plaster mold taken from the model. A cliché is a struck piece made from either the obverse or the reverse die for a two-sided piece. Clichés are made for the artist's own collection or for museums, for the purpose of display. The term gilt is used here to describe pieces which are either gold-plated or gilded. A single dimension indicates the diameter for a round piece. For rectangular pieces, the measurement of the height is given before the width. For irregular pieces, the same order is followed, with the maximum dimensions for the piece being given.

All pieces in the catalogue are understood to be from the ANS collection except where otherwise specified. Two credit lines for ANS pieces require explanation: "Eidlitz bequest" is abbreviated from "bequest of Mr. R. J. Eidlitz and gift of Mrs. R. J. Eidlitz; "J. Coolidge Hills collection bequest" refers to a collection of medals transferred to the ANS from the Wadsworth Atheneum (Hartford, Connecticut) by bequest of J. Coolidge Hills. All pieces illustrated in the catalogue are from the ANS collection, with the exception of John Flanagan's Rostron/*Titanic* Lifesaving Medal (***154***), which was photographed by permission of The Newark Museum. In the text and catalogue entries, italicized numbers indicate the pieces that are illustrated. Wherever possible medals are illustrated at full scale. Dimensions for medals illustrated at a reduced scale are given in the catalogue.

For the abbreviated bibliographical references that appear in the catalogue entries, the reader is referred to either the specific bibliography listed in that section of the catalogue or the general bibliography at the end of the catalogue.

The Renaissance of the Medal in France

Pierre-Jean David d'Angers (1788-1856)

The son of a sculptor, Pierre-Jean David d'Angers began his art studies at the drawing school in Angers, his birthplace. He also studied painting with a local Angevin artist before moving to Paris in 1808. In Paris, he studied with the sculptor Roland. David won the Grand Prix de Rome for sculpture in 1811 and spent three years at the French Academy in Rome. After his return to Paris, he pursued a standard academic career as a sculptor and was rewarded with a professorship at the Ecole des Beaux-Arts in 1826.

Beginning in 1827, David d'Angers embarked on a vast new project, the creation of the hundreds of portrait medallions that were to make up his "Gallery of Famous Men," planned as an "enduring didactic encyclopedia." Departing from the neo-Classical style of his earlier sculpture, David applied the tenets of the Romantic writers and painters to medallic portraiture, replacing the traditional engraved medal with direct, vigorously modeled "sketches in bronze." His posthumous portraits of the Romantic heroes Géricault (**1**) and Byron (***2***) demonstrate the expressive potential of his new style. The deliberately distorted features of the Byron portrait—the elongated skull, lofty brow, deep-set, dreamy eyes, and tousled hair—are typical of David's portraiture and show his interest in the correlation between physiognomy and genius.

BIBLIOGRAPHY: François Bergot, *David d'Angers*, Paris Mint exhibition catalogue (Paris, 1966); A. Bruel, ed., *Les carnets de David d'Angers* (Paris, 1958); Forrer, vol. 1, pp. 522-35, vol. 7, pp. 210-11; James Holderbaum, "Pierre-Jean David d'Angers," pp. 211-26 in *Romantics to Rodin*; Jones, pp. 110-12, 114; Henri Jouin, *David d'Angers, sa vie, son oeuvre, ses écrits et ses contemporains* (Paris, 1878); Lami, vol. 2, pp. 53-117; Marx 1897, pp. 11-12; Marx 1901, pl. 8; Henry de Morant, *David d'Angers et son temps* (Angers, 1956).

1. **Théodore Géricault, Painter, 1830**
   Cast bronze (uniface), 150 mm
   Bergot 121, pp. 102-3; *Romantics to Rodin* 93

2. **Lord Byron, 1830-1832**
   Cast bronze (uniface), 130 mm
   Bergot 143, pp. 114-17; *Romantics to Rodin* 95k

2

Henri Chapu (1833-1891)

Born in Le Mée, Henri Chapu moved with his family to Paris at the age of ten and was apprenticed two years later to an interior designer. Having completed the drawing course at the Petite Ecole, he was accepted in 1849 at the Ecole des Beaux-Arts, where he studied with the sculptors Pradier and Duret. In 1855 he was awarded the Grand Prix de Rome for sculpture, and he worked in Rome for five years before returning to Paris in 1861. Chapu was a professor at the Académie Julian in Paris for many years and also taught a modeling class in the night school at the Ecole des Beaux-Arts, although he never headed one of the ateliers there.

While he was primarily a sculptor of statues and monuments, Chapu, like many of the sculptors of his generation, also produced cast portrait medallions in the tradition of David. In comparison with David's forceful, Romantic portraits, Chapu's medallic portraiture, illustrated here by his portrait of the architect Guillaume (***3***), is more restrained and academic. The refined, low relief modeling of the Guillaume portrait marks a major change from both the hard-edged neo-Classical style and the bold relief of David's medallic portraits. Although the portrait of Guillaume is classical in format, the head, softly shaped by the play of light and shade across the subtly varied surface of the relief, is far from the cold, lifeless profiles of official neo-Classical portraiture.

BIBLIOGRAPHY: Benedite, p. 151; O. Fidière, *Chapu: sa vie et son oeuvre* (Paris, 1894); Forrer, vol. 1, pp. 407-10; June E. Hargrove, "Henri Chapu," pp. 172-74 in *Romantics to Rodin*; Lami, vol. 1, pp. 328-42; Marx 1897, pp. 12-13; Marx 1901, pl. 8.

3. **E. Guillaume, Architect, Rome 1861**
Cast bronze (uniface), 99 mm
Eidlitz bequest
Eidlitz 485

4. E. Vaudremer, undated
Cast bronze (uniface), 177 mm
Eidlitz bequest
Eidlitz 1008

Jules-Clément Chaplain (1839-1909)

Jules-Clément Chaplain was born in Mortagne and, after preparatory training, was admitted to the Ecole des Beaux-Arts in Paris in 1857. At the Ecole, he studied medal engraving under Oudiné and sculpture with Jouffroy and, in 1863, won the Grand Prix de Rome for medal engraving. After further study in Italy from 1864 to 1868, he returned to Paris, where he pursued an extremely successful career as a medalist, receiving numerous awards for his work at the Paris Salons and Universal Expositions. In 1877 Chaplain became the official medalist of the French government and, four years later, was elected to the prestigious Académie des Beaux-Arts.

As his biography suggests, Chaplain's work bridges the neo-Classical and Beaux-Arts traditions. In his cast portrait medals, such as those of Jeanne Mathilde Claude (***9***) and the painter Ernest Meissonier (***14***), the balance of bold linear definition and lively surface modeling creates a powerfully immediate, yet restrained, image of the sitter. The strong, simple outline of Madame Claude's profile gives the portrait an air of classical nobility, offset by the vigorously modeled drapery folds and the realistic treatment of her ample figure and garment.

The Meissonier medal belongs to a great series of portrait medals by Chaplain of the prominent French artists of his day. Inspired by the Romantic image of the artist, these portraits share some of the visionary intensity of David's medallic portraits, tempered by the sober draftsmanship and carefully finished modeling characteristic of Chaplain's work. In contrast to the dynamic obverse portraits, the reverses of most of these medals are disappointingly lifeless and academic.

Some of Chaplain's later medals are closer in style to the soft, pictorial work of his student Roty, although they retain the clear linear definition typical of the master's work. The reverse of Chaplain's beautiful medal commemorating the visit of the Russian fleet to Toulon in 1893 (***11***), with its pictorial treatment of the theme of France welcoming the Russian fleet, shows the influence of Roty, while the obverse, with its simple, refined jugate busts personifying France and Russia, is more classical in spirit. Chaplain's use of the rectangular format for some of his later portrait medals is likewise borrowed from Roty, although the style of portraiture in works like his 1899 plaquette honoring Louis Liard, the Director of Higher Education in France (**15**), is clearly his own.

14

BIBLIOGRAPHY: Benedite, pp. 148-50; Forrer, vol. 1, pp. 398-407, vol. 7, p. 179; IECM, pp. 49-56; Jones, pp. 120-22; Marx 1897, p. 8, pl. 3; Marx 1898, pls. 3-6; Marx 1901, pls. 11-14; Lami, vol. 1, pp. 320-26; F. Mazerolle, "J.-C. Chaplain; biographie et catalogue de

11

son oeuvre," *Gazette numismatique française* 1 (1897), pp. 7-42, 3 (1899), pp. 83-88, and 4 (1900), pp. 193-96.

5. Theodore Dwight Woolsey, 1881
Yale University
Struck bronze (Paris Mint), 68 mm
Gift of Ellen B. Streckel
Mazerolle 23

6. Siege of Paris (1870-1871), 1885
Struck silver (Paris Mint), 73 mm
Cat. gen., p. 74A; Dompierre de Chaufepié, p. 14; IECM 44; Mazerolle 30

7. Jean-Léon Gérôme, 1885
Cast bronze, 102 mm
Dompierre de Chaufepié, p. 72; IECM 24; Mazerolle 60

8. Henri d'Orleans, Duc d'Aumale, 1887
Cast bronze (uniface), 113 mm
IECM 22; Mazerolle 66

***9.* Jeanne Mathilde Claude, 1887**
Cast model for medal (uniface), bronze, 234 mm
Dompierre de Chaufepié, p. 14; IECM 31; Mazerolle 65

10. National School of Industrial Arts at Roubaix, 1890
Struck (Paris Mint): bronze, 69 mm; silvered bronze, 69 mm
Silvered bronze, Eidlitz bequest
Cat. gen., p. 79E; Dompierre de Chaufepié, p. 66; Mazerolle 39

***11.* Visit of the Russian Fleet to Toulon, 1893**
Struck (Paris Mint): bronze, 70 mm; silvered bronze, 70 mm
Gift of the Institut Français and gift of Daniel M. Friedenberg
Cat. gen., pp. 76-77D; Mazerolle 45

12. Smithsonian Institution Hodgkins Medal, 1896
Struck bronze (Paris Mint), 75 mm
Gift of Dr. F. W. Clark
AJN 34 (1899/1900), pp. 44-45; Mazerolle 50

13. Louise Davout, Marquise de Blocqueville, 1898
Struck silver (Paris Mint), 61 x 71 mm
Mazerolle 115

***14.* Ernest Meissonier, 1899**
Cast bronze, 99 mm
Dompierre de Chaufepié, p. 14; IECM 20; Mazerolle 126

15. Louis Liard, 1899
Struck (Paris Mint): bronze, 70 x 54 mm; silver, 70 x 54 mm
Cat. gen., p. 78D; Dompierre de Chaufepié, p. 73; Mazerolle 129

16. Victor Hugo Centennial, 1902
Struck silver (Paris Mint), 50 mm
Eidlitz bequest
IECM 48

Alexandre Louis Marie Charpentier (1856-1909)

Born in Paris, Alexandre Charpentier began his career by serving an apprenticeship to an engraver. He later worked as an assistant to the medalist Ponscarme and then entered the Ecole des Beaux-Arts, where he competed unsuccessfully for the Prix de Rome in medal engraving. Charpentier was active also in the decorative arts, collaborating with artisans to produce clocks, boxes, furniture and other objects ornamented with sculptural relief. In 1892-93 he joined other artists in founding the group "Les Cinq," dedicated to fostering the integration of the fine and applied arts.

Charpentier's work is unique among the French school of medalists for its naturalism and sculptural technique. His direct, roughly modeled portrait "sketches" (**17**) and more finished decorative plaques represent an adaptation of the sculptural idiom of Rodin to the art of the medal. The unidealized, dancing nude figure of Danseuse I (***21***) from 1907, captured in a fleeting, contorted pose, is a far cry from the timeless, elegant, allegorical nudes of the academic tradition.

As Mark Jones has pointed out, Charpentier's commissioned medals are more conventionally modeled in soft, low relief, but the social realism of some of these works marks a further departure from the Beaux-Arts school. His medal for the firm of Janvier and Duval (***23***) and his Stonemasons medal (**26**), for example, depict contemporary laborers in carefully observed detail, highlighting their physical strength and skill.

BIBLIOGRAPHY: Forrer, vol. 1, pp. 411-14, vol. 7, pp. 176-78; IECM, pp. 57-65; Jones, pp. 128-30; Lami, vol. 1, pp. 350-57; Marx 1897, pp. 30-31, pl. 10; Marx 1898, pls. 25-26; Marx 1901, pls. 15-16; Gabriel Mourey, "Some Recent Work by Alexandre Charpentier," *The Studio* 16 (1899), pp. 25-30.

17. Emile Zola, 1898
Cast bronze (uniface), 180 x 138 mm
Cat. gen., p. 83H

21

23

18. Hommage à Emile Zola, 1898
Struck bronze, 32 mm
AJN 34 (1899/1900), p. 58; Cat. gen., p. 84A; *The Numismatist* 11 (1898), pp. 249-50; *The Studio* 14 (1898), pp. 140, 143

19. Thérèse, 1899
Struck bronze (Paris Mint), 80 x 52 mm
Gift of Daniel M. Friedenberg
Dompierre de Chaufepié, vol. 2, p. 86

20. Société des Amis de la Médaille Française, 1901
Octagonal, struck bronze (Paris Mint), 66 x 72 mm
Dompierre de Chaufepié, vol. 2, p. 86; IECM, p. 307, no. 7

***21*. Danseuse I, 1907**
Cast bronze (uniface), 137 x 97 mm
IECM 5

22. Claude Debussy, 1907
Struck bronze (uniface), 57 mm

***23*. Janvier et Duval, 1908**
Octagonal, struck bronze (uniface), 53 x 60 mm
IECM 15

24. Jeux et Arts I (Painting), undated
Cast bronze (uniface), 84 x 154 mm
IECM 16

25. Jeux et Arts IV (Sculpture), undated
Cast bronze (uniface), 84 x 154 mm
IECM 19

26. Stonemasons, undated
Struck (Paris Mint): bronze, 74 x 61 mm; silver, 74 x 61 mm
Eidlitz bequest

27. Tuilerie d'Ivry (Emile Muller Co.), undated
Octagonal, cast bronze (uniface), 97 x 64 mm
IECM 31

Louis Oscar Roty (1846-1911)

Louis Oscar Roty, a native Parisian, was apprenticed as a youth to an engraver and chaser. After preliminary study at the Petite Ecole, he was admitted to the Ecole des Beaux-Arts in 1864. He initially studied painting, but later took up sculpture in the the atelier of Augustin Dumont. He also studied independently with the sculptor Henri Chapu and the medalists Ponscarme and Chaplain. In 1875 Roty won the Grand Prix de Rome for medal engraving and spent three years in Rome before returning to Paris. From that time on he did much to promote the art of the medal, and his work, exhibited regularly in the Paris Salons and Universal Expositions, was awarded the highest honors. Roty joined Chaplain as a member of the Académie des Beaux-Arts in 1888, after his former teacher urged his election in exception to the rule that only one medalist might hold a chair in the Académie.

Roty's training in drawing and painting is evident in his medallic work which displays a unique pictorial sensibility. His revival of the rectangular plaquette format in 1880 facilitated the innovative blending of sculpture and painting in his medals, allowing him to treat the medal essentially as a miniature picture in relief. For a portrait plaquette of his parents sculpted in 1886 (***28***), Roty employed a standard Renaissance composition, the double portrait with facing busts, but the contemporary dress and down-to-earth realism of his portrayal of the elderly Rotys make it clear that they are not Renaissance nobles. The candid detail and soft, painterly style of the relief gives the portraits an intimate, affectionate quality previously associated more with painting than with the public, official art of the medal.

Roty's famous plaquette commemorating the death and funeral of French President Sadi Carnot (***35***) shows the full potential of his style. Through the masterful handling of the devices of pictorial perspective, including the subtle gradation of the low relief so that objects meant to seem far away are in extremely low relief with finely incised details, Roty creates the illusion of a vast expanse. On the obverse, France is depicted mourning the dead Carnot, whose home appears far off in the distance. On the reverse, a group of veiled female figures carries the President's body towards its final resting place in the Pantheon. The empty space which surrounds the austere, solemn, allegorical figures

28

heightens the powerful emotion of the scenes. The figures themselves, with their classical restraint, have been compared to Greek statuary, and the careful drapery studies in the tradition of Ingres (which exist for this piece and many of Roty's other medals) bear out this analogy.

The popularity of his medals brought Roty a number of commissions for portrait medals of prominent Americans. His commemorative medal of Baltimore financier William Thompson Walters (***34***) presents further evidence of the artist's talent as a portraitist. The reverse of this medal, however, illustrates the complaint sometimes leveled against Roty's work that his pictorial compositions are too fussy and inappropriate to the scale of the medium. Here Roty uses a characteristic landscape vista to give an artificial sense of cohesion to the wealth of information about Walters which he provides, but the meaning of the imagery is somewhat obscure. In the foreground, a caduceus, perhaps intended to symbolize the railroad which formed the basis of Walters' fortune, rests against a large tree, the illogical focal point of the composition. Behind the tree is a sculpture of a lion inscribed with the name BARYE, a reference to Walters' role in providing for a monument in Paris to the French sculptor Barye, whose work he avidly collected. The cities of Harrisburg, Pennsylvania (Walters' birthplace), and Baltimore (his place of residence) appear in the distant background.

35

BIBLIOGRAPHY: Benedite, pp. 162-66; Dompierre de Chaufepié, pp. 19-26; Forrer, vol. 5, pp. 228-49, vol. 8, pp. 175-78, 359; IECM, pp. 267-75; Jones, pp. 121-25; George F. Kunz, "The Late Louis Oscar Roty: His Life Work and His Influence on the Past and Future of Medallic Art," *AJN* 47 (1913), pp. 93-119; Marx 1897, pp. 20-23, pls. 6-7; Marx 1898, pls. 12-16; Marx 1901, pls. 17-19; F. Mazerolle, "L. O. Roty, membre de l'Institut: biographie et catalogue de son oeuvre," *Gazette numismatique française* 1 (1897), pp. 129-56 and 451-69, 2 (1898), pp. 401-4, and 9 (1905), pp. 225-38; E. B. S., "Oscar Roty and the Art of the Medallist," *The Studio* 7 (1896), pp. 158-62.

***28.* Parents of the Artist, 1886**
Cast silvered bronze (uniface), 136 x 151 mm

Gift of Georges Roty
Dompierre de Chaufepié, p. 21; Mazerolle 110

29. Maurice Roty, 1886
Cast bronze, 66 x 49 mm

Eidlitz bequest
Dompierre de Chaufepié, p. 21; IECM 60; Mazerolle 100

30. Franco-American Union, 1886
Struck (Paris Mint): bronze, 68 mm; silvered bronze, 68 mm

Bronze, gift of Rev. Foster Ely, D.D.
Cat. gen., p. 358C; Dompierre de Chaufepié, p. 20; IECM 80; Mazerolle 11

31. East Algerian Railway, 1886
Struck (Paris Mint): silver, 68 mm; cast bronze, 100 mm

Bequest of A. Carson Simpson and gift of Georges Roty
Dompierre de Chaufepié, p. 21; IECM 12; Mazerolle 13, 109

32. Michel-Eugène Chevreul, 1886
Struck (Paris Mint): bronze, 68 mm; silver, 68 mm

Gift of Georges Roty and gift of Daniel M. Friedenberg
Dompierre de Chaufepié, p. 21; IECM 64; Cat. gen., p. 359D; Mazerolle 12

33. 50th Anniversary of the Christofle Firm, 1893
Struck (Paris Mint): silver, 59 x 95 mm; gilt bronze, 59 x 95 mm

Gift of Albert M. Kohn and Eidlitz bequest
Dompierre de Chaufepié, p. 24; IECM 13; Mazerolle 54

34. William Thompson Walters, 1896
Cast bronze (uniface), 116 mm; struck bronze, 117 mm

Gift of Georges Roty and Eidlitz bequest
Lillian C. Randall, ed., *The Diary of George A. Lucas: An American Art Agent in Paris, 1857-1909* (Princeton, 1979), vol. 2, pp. 814, 825, and 830

35. Death of President Sadi Carnot, 1898
Cast bronze (uniface), reverse, 259 x 186 mm; struck silver (Paris Mint), 80 x 56 mm

Silver, gift of Daniel M. Friedenberg
Dompierre de Chaufepié, pp. 25-26; IECM 72; Cat. gen., p. 358A; Mazerolle 156

36. Mines of Lens, 1899
Struck silver (Paris Mint), 67 x 48 mm

Mazerolle 177; Stahl, p. 2068

37. Inauguration of the Prison of Fresnes-les-Rungis, 1900
Struck (Paris Mint): bronze, 58 x 79 mm; silver, 58 x 79 mm

Silver, Eidlitz bequest
Dompierre de Chaufepié, p. 79; IECM 41, Mazerolle 174

38. Abram Stevens Hewitt/Rapid Transit, 1900
New York State Chamber of Commerce
Struck (Tiffany & Co.): bronze, 68 mm; silver, 68 mm

Mazerolle 188

34

39. Phoebe Hearst, 1901
International Competition for the Architectural Plan of the University of California
Cast bronze (uniface), reverse, 140 x 108 mm; struck bronze (Paris Mint), 79 x 60 mm

Eidlitz bequest and gift of Georges Roty
Eidlitz 68, 69; Mazerolle 191

40. Dr. Paul Brouardel, 1902
Struck silver (Paris Mint), 70 x 50 mm

Gift of Georges Roty
IECM 19; Mazerolle 194

41. Peter Cooper, 1909
50th Anniversary of the Cooper Union
Struck (Tiffany & Co.): bronze, 68 mm; silver, 68 mm

Kunz, p. 101

Louis Alexandre Bottée (1852-1941)

Louis Alexandre Bottée was born in Paris and apprenticed at age thirteen to a button maker, where he learned the art of engraving. He began his art studies in the evening classes of the Paris drawing schools and later attended the Petite Ecole. In 1869 he entered the atelier of the chief Parisian medal engraver, Tasset, and in 1871 he was accepted to study with the medalist Ponscarme at the Ecole des Beaux-Arts. After winning the Grand Prix de Rome for medal engraving in 1878, Bottée spent three years at the French Academy in Rome. When he returned to Paris, his work was well received, and he was awarded honors at the Paris Salons.

As his training suggests, Bottée's work epitomizes the French academic tradition of his day. His medals, such as the one commemorating the opening of the Port of Tunis in 1893 (***43***), generally feature elaborate allegorical compositions, modeled in the soft style developed by Roty. In comparison with similar compositions by Roty (**31**, for example), the greater flamboyance of Bottée's style is apparent. On the exuberant reverse of the Tunis medal, a nude woman bearing a cornucopia and a sprig of laurel is depicted rising from the waves on the back of a hybrid sea monster, with the port dimly visible in the distance. The entire composition is filled with dynamic movement, generated by the swirling line and the active poses of the figures.

BIBLIOGRAPHY: Benedite, pp. 146-47; Forrer, vol. 1, pp. 229-33, vol. 7, p. 103, vol. 8, p. 320; IECM, pp. 16-23; Marx 1897, pl. 8; Marx 1898, pls. 17-18.

42. République Française, 1887
Cast model for medal (uniface), bronze, 232 mm
IECM 33

***43.* Inauguration of the Port of Tunis, 1893**
Struck silvered bronze (Paris Mint), 68 mm
IECM 22

44. Centenary of the Paris Natural History Museum, 1893
Struck bronze (Paris Mint), 69 mm
Cat. gen., p. 61E

45. Société des Architectes Diplomés, 1896
Struck (Paris Mint): gilt bronze, 71 mm; silvered bronze, 71 mm
Eidlitz bequest
IECM 35

46. Centenary of the Internships in Medicine and Surgery, 1902
Hôpitaux Civils de Paris
Struck bronze (Paris Mint), 68 mm
Cat. gen., p. 61F; IECM 6

47. Léon Louis Davoust, Architect, 1904
Cast bronze (uniface), 119 mm
Eidlitz bequest
Eidlitz 847

48. Aux poètes morts sans gloire, 1904
Struck bronze (Paris Mint), 90 mm
Gift of Daniel M. Friedenberg
IECM 4

49. Resurrection of San Francisco, 1906
Struck bronze (Paris Mint), 90 mm
Cat. gen., p. 60C; IECM 34

43

Nineteenth-Century American Medals

53

Charles Cushing Wright (1796-1854)

Born in Damariscotta, Maine, C. C. Wright taught himself engraving as an apprentice to John Osburn, a jeweler and watchmaker in Utica, New York. After working for a number of years as an itinerant engraver, Wright settled in New York City, where he established a die engraving firm in partnership with James Bale. In 1840 he went into the bank note engraving business with the artist Asher B. Durand and later became one of the founding members of the National Academy of Design and lectured there on the art of the medal.

Although executed in the prevailing neo-Classical style of the period, Wright's strongly individualized portraits of the prominent civic leaders and artists of America's early years rise above the bland idealism often associated with that style. His skill as a die engraver is apparent in the detail of his portraits of Daniel Webster (*53*) and Henry Clay (**54**), which follow Roman models in the exaggerated realism of their boldly indicated wrinkles and veins. Working within the established format of official, neo-Classical medals, Wright adds visual interest to the Clay and Webster medals through his careful attention to inscriptions and decorative borders. While he often engraved his medals from reliefs modeled by other artists, the noble portrait of Webster is his own design, as are the innovative pictorial reverses of the Webster and Clay medals. The reverse of the Webster medal, which features an imaginary monument to the statesman with the U.S. Capitol as it appeared at the time in the distance, is particularly noteworthy for its balanced composition and fine detail.

BIBLIOGRAPHY: "Charles Cushing Wright, Distinguished Medalist," pp. 67-68 in Chamberlain; Forrer, vol. 6, pp. 556-57; "Medallions of America's Old Masters," pp. 11-14 in Chamberlain.

50. Will Page, 1843
Modeled by Salathiel Ellis
Struck bronze (U.S. Mint), 48 mm

Eidlitz bequest
Julian PE-24

51. Gilbert Stuart, 1848
American Art Union

Obverse modeled by Salathiel Ellis; reverse modeled by Duggan
Struck (U.S. Mint): bronze, 65 mm; white metal, 65 mm

Chamberlain, pp. 12-13, fig. 7; Julian PE-3

52. George Washington/Declaration of Independence, undated (circa 1851)
Reverse after painting by John Trumbull
Struck bronze, 90 mm

W. S. Baker, *Medallic Portraits of Washington* (Philadelphia, 1885; rpt., Iola, Wisc., 1965), pp. 32, 34, no. 53; Chamberlain, fig. 4; Rulau and Fuld, pp. 54-55

53. **Daniel Webster, 1852**
Struck bronze, 76 mm

Eidlitz bequest
Chamberlain, fig. 7; Julian PE-37

54. **Henry Clay, undated (after 1852)**
Struck bronze, 76 mm

Chamberlain, fig. 33; Julian PE-8

Anthony C. Paquet (1814-1882)

A native of Hamburg, Germany, Anthony C. Paquet came to America in 1848 and settled in Philadelphia. From 1857 until 1864, he was assistant engraver at the U.S. Mint in Philadelphia, where he designed a number of the official medals awarded for acts of bravery by authorization of Congress (**56** and ***59***, for example). In his re-evaluation of these medals, Cornelius Vermeule has stressed the "Victorian grandeur" of Paquet's figural compositions, resulting from the artist's investment of neo-Classical forms with the "lofty sentiment" characteristic of his era. Vermeule draws a convincing parallel between the tableaux-like compositions of Paquet's medals, such as the one honoring the rescuers of victims from the wreck of the steamship *San Francisco* (***59***), and the popular re-enactments of such events on the stage or in the patriotic parades of the day. The dramatic vignette on the obverse of the *San Francisco* Lifesaving Medal, which depicts a man and woman adrift on a raft threatened by churning waves, with a rescue ship appearing far off in the distance, is the epitome of Victorian sentiment.

BIBLIOGRAPHY: Forrer, vol. 4, p. 381, vol. 7, p. 109; Vermeule, pp. 79-81.

55. **James Ross Snowden, 1859**
Restrike (U.S. Mint), bronze, 80 mm

Gift of Bauman L. Belden
Julian MT-3; U.S. Mint 1972, no. 303; Vermeule, pp. 79-80

56. **James Buchanan/Lifesaving Medal to Dr. Frederick Rose, 1861**
By act of U.S. Congress
Struck bronze (U.S. Mint), 76 mm

Julian PE-29; Loubat 69, pp. 362-63; U.S. Mint 1972, no. 618

57. **Philadelphia Sanitary Fair, 1864**
Struck bronze (U.S. Mint), 58 mm

Julian CM-44

58. **Andrew Johnson Indian Peace Medal, 1865**
Struck (U.S. Mint): bronze, 76 mm; white metal, 76 mm

Indian Peace Medals 55; Julian IP-40; Loubat 75, p. 410; Vermeule, pp. 79-80

59. **SS *San Francisco* Lifesaving Medal, 1866**
By act of U.S. Congress
Restrike (U.S. Mint), bronze, 81 mm

Julian LS-11; Loubat 76, p. 411; U.S. Mint 1972, no. 525; Vermeule, p. 81

William Barber (1807-1879) and Charles E. Barber (1840-1917)

The Barbers, father and son, were both born in London, where William was trained in engraving by his father, John Barber. Before he immigrated

59

62

to America, the older Barber worked as a die engraver for the De La Rue firm in London. In 1852 he moved his family to Boston, where they lived for ten years, until he was hired by Gorham & Co. as an engraver of dies for the ornamental embossing of silver plate. William Barber became assistant engraver at the U.S. Mint in Philadelphia in 1865, and he was promoted in 1869 to the position of Chief Mint Engraver. At that time his son, Charles E. Barber, was employed as assistant engraver, and he replaced his father as head engraver after the latter's death in 1879.

A series of portrait medals signed with the initials of both Barbers (**61**, ***62***, **63**) feature classicizing heads similar to those by C. C. Wright, but of a more generalized nature. Vermeule singles out for criticism the Barbers' idealized, Greco-Roman portrait of Ulysses S. Grant (***62***) on the medal issued in 1879 to commemorate his presidency. No sense of the General's personality is conveyed by this portrait, and the inappropriate, heavy "Pseudo-Gothic" lettering of the inscription which surrounds the head further weakens the design. Charles Barber's Benjamin Harrison inaugural medal (***65***), issued a decade after the Grant medal, features the same archaizing Gothic lettering and a similar unimaginative foliate wreath on the reverse, but the more realistic bust portrait of Harrison in civilian dress on the obverse of this medal marks an improvement over the Barbers' classicizing portrayal of Grant. The deeply undercut high relief of the Harrison portrait gives this image a forcefulness which was lacking in the Grant portrait.

BIBLIOGRAPHY: Forrer, vol. 1, pp. 122-23, vol. 7, pp. 45-46; Vermeule, pp. 82-85; "William Barber," *AJN* 14 (1879/80), pp. 55-56.

60. U.S. Grant/Union Pacific Railway, 1869
William Barber
Struck (U.S. Mint): bronze, 45 mm; silver, 45 mm
Bronze, bequest of A. Carson Simpson
Julian CM-39; U.S. Mint 1972, no. 623

61. W. H. Furness, 1875
William and Charles Barber
Struck bronze (U.S. Mint), 64 mm
Eidlitz bequest
Julian PE-12

***62.* Ulysses S. Grant, 1879**
William and Charles Barber
Struck bronze (U.S. Mint), 76 mm
J. Coolidge Hills collection bequest
Julian PR-15; U.S. Mint 1972, no. 118; Vermeule, p. 82

63. Joseph Henry, 1879
William and Charles Barber
Struck bronze (U.S. Mint), 64 mm
Eidlitz bequest
Julian PE-14

64. National Exposition of Railway Appliances, Chicago, 1883
Charles E. Barber and George T. Morgan
Struck: silver, 58 mm; bronze, 58 mm
Bequest of A. Carson Simpson and bequest of James B. Nies

***65.* Benjamin Harrison Inaugural Medal, 1889**
Charles E. Barber
Struck bronze (U.S. Mint), 77 mm
Gift of Elizabeth Mann
Julian PR-24; U.S. Mint 1972, no. 123; Vermeule, pp. 84-85

65

66. Benjamin Harrison Indian Peace Medal, 1889
Charles E. Barber and George T. Morgan
Oval, struck bronze (U.S. Mint), 76 x 60 mm

Greenwood collection gift
Indian Peace Medals 62; Julian IP-47; U.S. Mint 1972, no. 632

Louis Saint-Gaudens (1854-1913)

Born in New York, Louis Saint-Gaudens worked as a studio assistant to his famous older brother from 1872 until Augustus' death in 1907. Although he is credited with few independent works, Louis played a major role in the execution of his brother's sculptures. The Congressional medal presented to Joseph Francis in 1890 (***67***) for his contributions to the technology and organization of the U.S. Lifesaving Service is attributed to Louis Saint-Gaudens. Although the literature on this piece is unclear, it seems that he was responsible for preparing the models for the medal, perhaps from a design by Zeleima Jackson. His use of a composition in the tradition of earlier American lifesaving medals for the reverse, while relying on more contemporary sources for the design of the obverse, would best explain the jarring difference in style between the two sides of the medal. The obverse of the Francis medal, with its vigorously modeled, naturalistic bust portrait, Renaissance format, and border of stars, closely resembles the obverse of Augustus Saint-Gaudens' important medal for the George Washington Inaugural Centennial of 1889 (***77***). Executed in a more wooden, two-dimensional style, the vignette of a sea rescue on the reverse of the Francis medal, typical of nineteenth century American lifesaving medals, has the character of a folk-art painting.

BIBLIOGRAPHY: Gardner, pp. 63-64.

67. **Life Saving Medal to Joseph Francis, 1889/90**
By act of the U.S. Congress
Struck bronze (U.S. Mint), 105 mm; restrike (U.S. Mint), bronze, 76 mm

Julian LS-13; U.S. Mint 1972, no. 637

Olin Levi Warner (1844-1896)

Olin Levi Warner was born in West Suffield, Connecticut, and grew up in Amsterdam, New York. At the age of fifteen he received his first art instruction at a private school in Florida which he attended for two years. After he returned to live with his family in Vermont, Warner pursued his interest in sculpture on his own and worked for six years as a telegrapher to save enough money for study in Paris. He left for Paris in 1869 and was admitted to the atelier of Jouffroy at the Ecole des Beaux-Arts in the spring of 1870, following preliminary study at the Petite Ecole. Before his return to America in 1872, he also worked for several months as an assistant in the studio of Jean-Baptiste Carpeaux, the foremost French decorative sculptor at the time.

After he came back to New York, Warner struggled for a number of years to establish his career, but finally achieved some critical success with

67

his portrait busts and medallions. His numerous portrait medallions, which should be recognized as the earliest works of American medallic art to reflect the development of the cast medal in France, bear a resemblance to the medallions of David d'Angers in both format and technique. According to George Gurney, Warner's regard for David's work is also attested by his Paris sketchbook, where several pages are filled with a list of the portrait medals by David which he must have seen at the Louvre. Warner's medallions of his friend Thomas Fenton (**68**) and his parents (**69**), executed in 1878 and 1879 respectively, are comparable to medallions by David in their bold relief, vigorous modeling and hastily scrawled inscriptions, but a simple naturalism replaces the Romantic distortions of David's portraiture. The Fenton medallion, with its classical air and softly textured modeling, might in fact more aptly be compared with Chapu's medallic portraiture (*3*).

Among the finest of Warner's medallions are the series of eight portraits of Northwest Indians which he modeled from life on three trips to Oregon and Idaho between 1889 and 1891, arranged by his friend Col. C. E. S. Wood. The portraits of Chief Joseph (**70**), "Young Chief" (*71*), and Sabina (**72**) all share the spare format of a profile bust flanked by simple, vertical inscriptions, which focuses attention on the artist's masterful modeling. Warner's realistic treatment of these portraits, which exhibit a wide range of ages and facial types, shows his interest in providing an accurate ethnological record of the Northwest tribes, rather than creating the kind of generalized, symbolic Indian sculpted by many of his contemporaries. The "Young Chief" medallion, with its variety of textures and softly modulated relief, illustrates the sculptor's skillful use of light and shade to shape a strong likeness of the sitter. Warner's talent as a medalist was recognized a few years before his untimely death in the commission for the first U.S. commemorative coin, the Columbian half dollar (**82**), which will be discussed in a later section of this catalogue.

BIBLIOGRAPHY: W. C. Brownell, "The Sculpture of Olin Warner," *Scribner's Magazine* 20 (1896), pp. 429-41; Craven, pp. 406-9; Henry Eckford [Charles De Kay], "Olin Levi Warner, Sculptor," *The Century Magazine* 37 (1889), pp. 392-401; Gardner, pp. 40-45; George Gurney, "Olin Levi Warner (1844-1896): A Catalogue Raisonné of His Sculpture and Graphic Work," 3 vols., Ph.D. diss., University of Delaware, 1978; Paula M. Kozol, "Olin Levi Warner," pp. 201-5 in MFA 1986; Taft, pp. 268-76; Whitney 1976, p. 318; C. E. S. Wood, "Famous Indians, Portraits of Some American Chiefs," *The Century Magazine* 46 (1893), pp. 436-45.

71

68. Thomas Fenton, New York, 1878
Cast bronze (Tiffany & Co., 1897/8), uniface, 180 mm

The Metropolitan Museum of Art, 98.5.2 (gift of the National Sculpture Society, 1898)
Craven, p. 407; Gardner, p. 40; Gurney, vol. 2, pp. 389-90

69. The Artist's Parents, 1879
Cast bronze (uniface), 277 mm

The Metropolitan Museum of Art, 98.5.3 (gift of the National Sculpture Society, 1898)
Craven, p. 407; Eckford, pp. 394-95; Gardner, p. 40; Gurney, vol. 1, p. 82, vol. 2, pp. 392-94

70. "Joseph," Chief of the Nez Percé, 1889
Cast bronze (Jno. Williams Inc., N.Y.), uniface, 455 mm

Detroit 1983, pp. 261-62; Gurney, vol. 1, pp. 150-52, vol. 2, pp. 684-91; Wood, p. 436

***71.* "Young-Chief," Cayuse Indian, 1891**
Cast bronze (uniface), 184 mm

Gurney, vol. 2, pp. 731-33; Wood, p. 442

72. Sabina, Kash-Kash's Daughter, 1891
Cast bronze (Jno. Williams Inc., N.Y.), uniface, 147 mm

Gurney, vol. 2, pp. 734-35; Wood, p. 443.

Augustus Saint-Gaudens, Master of Relief

Augustus Saint-Gaudens (1848-1907)

Augustus Saint-Gaudens, the son of a French shoemaker and his Irish wife, was born in Dublin, Ireland. When he was six months old, the family immigrated to America and settled in New York. At the age of thirteen, he was apprenticed to a cameo cutter, a trade which he continued to practice while pursuing his formal art training in New York, Paris and Rome. Around 1864, Saint-Gaudens began studying drawing and modeling in evening classes at the Cooper Union and the National Academy of Design in New York. In 1867 he left for further studies in Paris, where he completed a preliminary course at the Petite Ecole before being accepted to the atelier of Jouffroy at the Ecole des Beaux-Arts. Forced to leave Paris in 1870 by the Franco-Prussian War, Saint-Gaudens went to Rome and set up his own studio there. During a visit to New York in 1875, he received several major commissions which he worked on in Paris between 1877 and 1880. In the 1880s, he was again in New York, and from 1885 on he spent his summers in Cornish, New Hampshire. He worked in Paris once again from 1897 until 1900, when he returned to the United States for the last time, settling in Cornish for the remaining years of his life. Saint-Gaudens taught for many years at the Art Students League in New York and trained a whole generation of younger sculptors as assistants in his busy studios.

Saint-Gaudens' training as a cameo cutter, his Parisian schooling in modeling, and his discovery of early Renaissance art in Italy laid the foundations for his innovations in relief sculpture, which in turn gave rise to the flowering of American medallic art in the first decades of the twentieth century. According to Homer Saint-Gaudens, his father's interest in working in low relief was sparked by a suggestion by his friend John LaFarge that he "paint a bas-relief," following the examples of the Quattrocento masters whom he greatly admired. Further inspired by Chapu's portrait medallions which he encountered on his return to Paris, Saint-Gaudens set about developing a new, vital style of relief modeling in a remarkable series of portrait reliefs that includes the 1879 portrait of the cosmopolitan American painter Francis Davis Millet (**73**) and the 1880 relief of French painter Jules Bastien-Lepage (***74***).

74

The portraits of Millet and Bastien-Lepage, modeled in the exquisite low relief which became a hallmark of Saint-Gaudens' style, demonstrate the artist's ability to "draw by means of light and shade...getting with an infinitesimal projection [of the relief] enough variety of shadow to convey a complete impression of nature" (Kenyon Cox). Both reliefs masterfully illustrate the sculptor's "chief maxim" of relief modeling, reported by his son Homer in the *Reminiscences*, "that the perfect relief texture, lettering, molding, background, and all, should interest by its color and light from edge to edge." In the Bastien-Lepage and Millet portraits, Saint-Gaudens characteristically works the identifying inscription into the composition as a decorative feature. The background, textured by fine linear striations which Kathryn Greenthal has compared with the lines of a print, also becomes part of the design, producing the effect of a soft atmosphere surrounding the figure.

Like a number of Saint-Gaudens' other portrait reliefs, including his famous portrait of Robert Louis Stevenson (***76***), the relief of Bastien-Lepage (***74***) was produced in many different versions, varied in size and detail to create a commercially successful series of limited editions. The Bastien-Lepage relief from the collection of the Boston Museum, probably an example of the first version of the piece, is a particularly fine cast, distinguished from later versions by the whimsical decorative motif at the upper left and the inclusion of Louis Saint-Gaudens' name in the inscription. The plaster mold from the collection of the Saint-Gaudens National Historic Site and the gilt bronze cast in the ANS collection represent a later reduced-scale edition of the Bastien-Lepage relief. Both the decrease in scale and the gold plating of the ANS piece somewhat obscure the subtle modeling of the relief, which Saint-Gaudens considered to be "as near perfection as he ever came."

Despite their relatively small number, Saint-Gaudens' medals, like his bas-reliefs, had an enormous impact on the development of American medallic art. His first official medal, for the New York celebration of the centennial of George Washington's inauguration (***77***), is also his most influential medallic work. Cornelius Vermeule has pointed out the many similarities between this piece and portrait medallions by the Quattrocento artist Pisanello, both in the balanced composition of the obverse and in the technique and the handling of lettering. Executed by Philip Martiny under Saint-Gaudens' close supervision, the Washington medal, with its lively modeled surfaces and elegant bust, was produced by casting in the tradition of Italian Renaissance medals, rather than by striking.

Saint-Gaudens received several other important commissions for medals in the course of his career, including the controversial award medal for the World's Columbian Exposition (***86*** and ***87***) and a special inaugural medal for President Theodore Roosevelt (***78***). The obverse of the Roosevelt medal is comparable in format to the obverse of the Washington medal, but the portrayal of the president in the later piece is less successful. The noble eagle on the reverse of the Roosevelt inaugural medal, skillfully modeled by Adolph A. Weinman, had been used earlier as part of the rejected design for the reverse of the Columbian Exposition medal and would be used again for the reverse of the new U.S. ten-dollar gold piece (***201***) at the request of President Roosevelt. Saint-Gaudens' design for the 1907 twenty-dollar gold piece (***202***), initially struck in high relief on a medal press, was his final and most beautiful medallic work.

Other less formal medals by Saint-Gaudens

78

attest to his sense of humor. He delighted in creating quick sketches or caricatures of his artist friends, such as the cast medallion of painter John Singer Sargent (***75***), with its Italian inscription BRUTTO RITRATTO ("bad" or "brutal" portrait), which may be a double entendre referring to the Roman Republican coins of Marcus Junius Brutus, as Vermeule suggests. In 1905/6 Saint-Gaudens modeled a charming plaquette (***79***) in low relief as a remembrance for his friends and neighbors who had staged an outdoor entertainment to celebrate the twentieth anniversary of his residence in Cornish. The theater curtains hung with ancient comic masks, the Roman temple, and the ancient bowl featured in the design all refer to the masque "The Gods and the Golden Bowl" which had been performed in honor of Augusta and Augustus Saint-Gaudens.

BIBLIOGRAPHY: Royal Cortissoz, *Augustus Saint-Gaudens* (Boston, 1907); Kenyon Cox, "Augustus Saint-Gaudens," *The Century Magazine* 35 (1887), pp. 28-37; Craven, pp. 373-92; John H. Dryfhout and Beverly Cox, *Augustus Saint-Gaudens: The Portrait Reliefs*, catalogue of an exhibition at the National Portrait Gallery (Washington, D.C., 1969); John H. Dryfhout, "Augustus Saint-Gaudens," and "Robert Louis Stevenson," pp. 181-86 and 187-200, in Jeanne L. Wasserman, ed., *Metamorphoses in Nineteenth-Century Sculpture* (Cambridge, Mass., 1975) and *The Work of Augustus Saint-Gaudens* (Hanover, NH, and London, 1982); Forrer, vol. 2, pp. 215-16, vol. 7, p. 343; Gardner, pp. 45-56; Kathryn Greenthal, *Augustus Saint-Gaudens, Master Sculptor* (New York, 1985) and "Augustus Saint-Gaudens," pp. 214-49 in MFA 1986; IECM, pp. 335, 338; Marx 1901, p. vii, pls. 28-29; Homer Saint-Gaudens, "The Later Works of Augustus Saint-Gaudens," *The Century Magazine* 75 (1908), pp. 695-713; Homer Saint-Gaudens, ed., *The Reminiscences of Augustus Saint-Gaudens*, 2 vols. (New York, 1913); B. H. Saxton, "Augustus Saint-Gaudens," *The Numismatist* 22 (1909), pp. 161-64; Taft, pp. 279-309; Louise Hall Tharp, *Saint-Gaudens and the Gilded Era* (Boston and Toronto, 1969); Vermeule, pp. 93-99, 109-11; Whitney 1976, pp. 306-7; Talcott Williams, "Augustus Saint-Gaudens," *The International Studio* 33 (1908), pp. cxxiii-cxxxviii.

79

73. **Francis Davis Millet, Paris, 1879**
Cast bronze (uniface), 264 x 174 mm

The Metropolitan Museum of Art, 10.223 (gift of Mrs. F. W. Adlard, 1910)
Dryfhout 1982, no. 78; Gardner, p. 46; MFA 1986, pp. 220-22; *Portrait Reliefs*, no. 13; *Reminiscences*, vol. 1, p. 214

74. **Jules Bastien-Lepage, Paris, 1880**
Cast bronze (uniface), 371 x 262 mm; cast (Gorham & Co.), uniface, gilt bronze, 160 x 115 mm; plaster mold, 165 x 115 mm

Bronze, Museum of Fine Arts, Boston, 81.39 (Everett Fund); plaster, Collection of the U.S. Dept. of the Interior, National Park Service, Saint-Gaudens National Historic Site, Cornish, N.H., no. 1177
Dryfhout 1982, no. 87; Greenthal 1985, pp. 91-92; MFA 1986, pp. 222-25, no. 67; *Portrait Reliefs*, no. 87; *Reminiscences*, vol. 1, pp. 215-17, 219

75. **John Singer Sargent, 1885**
Cast bronze (uniface), 62 mm; plaster mold, 95 x 87 mm

The Metropolitan Museum of Art, 13.78 (gift of Mrs. Edward Robinson, 1913) and collection of the U.S. Dept. of the Interior, National Park Service, Saint-Gaudens National Historic Site, Cornish, N.H., no. 1227
Dryfhout 1982, no. 86; Gardner, p. 56; MFA 1986, pp. 225-27; *Portrait Reliefs*, no. 19; *Reminiscences*, vol. 1, p. 250; Vermeule, p. 98

76. **Robert Louis Stevenson, 1887/8**
Cast bronze (after 1895, probably posthumous), uniface, 451 mm

Craven, p. 387; Dryfhout, "Robert Louis Stevenson"; Dryfhout 1982, no. 133; Greenthal 1985, pp. 119-21; *Portrait Reliefs*, no. 40; *Reminiscences*, vol. 1, pp. 373-89

77. George Washington Inaugural Centennial, 1889

Designed by Saint-Gaudens, modeled by Philip Martiny

Cast (Gorham & Co.): bronze, 114 mm; silver, 110 mm; plaster mold of obverse and reverse, 140 x 280 mm

Bronze, gift of Robert Weinman from the collection of Adolph A. Weinman; plaster, Collection of the U.S. Dept. of the Interior, National Park Service, Saint-Gaudens National Historic Site, Cornish, N.H., no. 3420

AJN 24 (1889/90), p. 35; Clarence W. Bowen, ed., *The History of the Centennial Celebration of the Inauguration of George Washington* (New York, 1892), pp. 138-41; Susan H. Douglas, "George Washington Medals of 1889," *The Numismatist* 62 (1949), p. 405, no. 53; Dryfhout 1982, no. 134; MacNeil 1977, pp. 41-45; MFA 1986, pp. 227-29; *Reminiscences*, vol. 1, pp. 391-93; Rulau and Fuld, pp. 214-15; B. H. Saxton, "Washington Medallion by Augustus Saint-Gaudens," *The Numismatist* 56 (1943), pp. 94-96; Vermeule, pp. 96-97

78. Theodore Roosevelt Special Inaugural Medal, 1905

Designed by Saint-Gaudens, modeled by A. A. Weinman

Cast bronze (Tiffany & Co.), 74 mm

AJN 40 (1905/6), p. 26; Dryfhout 1982, no. 197; MacNeil 1977, pp. 56-61; Frank Owen Payne, "More Roosevelt Sculptures," *Art and Archaeology* 8 (1919), pp. 199, 202; *Portrait Reliefs*, no. 55; *Reminiscences*, vol. 2, pp. 253-54; Vermeule, pp. 109-11

79. Cornish Masque Commemorative Plaquette, 1905/6

Struck (Tiffany & Co.), silvered bronze, 80 x 47 mm

Dryfhout 1982, no. 202; "Later Works," pp. 700, 711; *Reminiscences*, vol. 2, pp. 346-52

80. Victory Medallion, undated (circa 1905)

Cast bronze (uniface), 245 mm

Collection of the U.S. Dept. of the Interior, National Park Service, Saint-Gaudens National Historic Site, Cornish, N.H., no. 82

Dryfhout 1982, no. 205; "Later Works," p. 705; MFA 1986, pp. 248-49; *Reminiscences*, vol. 2, pp. 291-331

81. Benjamin Franklin Bicentennial, 1906

Initial design by Augustus Saint-Gaudens, final version by Louis Saint-Gaudens

Struck bronze cliché of obverse, original design, 100 mm; struck bronze (Tiffany & Co.), final version, 100 mm

AJN 41 (1907), p. 58; Melvin and George Fuld, "Medallic Memorials to Franklin," *The Numismatist* 69 (1956), pp.1420-22, FR.M.UN.6 and .7; B. H. Saxton, "The Franklin Bicentennial Medal," *The Numismatist* 69 (1956), pp. 1386-87

76

Exposition and Celebration

86

The World's Columbian Exposition, Chicago, 1892-1893

The World's Columbian Exposition heralded not only the coming of age of the Beaux-Arts style in American sculpture, but a major turning point in the history of American medallic and numismatic art as well. Hundreds of medals and tokens were issued by European and American firms as souvenirs of the World's Fair, and the first U.S. commemorative coins were minted and sold to help defray the cost of the Exposition. Olin Levi Warner and Augustus Saint-Gaudens, two of the premier American sculptors of the period, were engaged to design the commemorative half dollar (**82**) and the award medal for the Exposition (***86*** and ***87***). The choice of Warner to design the Columbian half dollar by the Board of Managers of the World's Columbian Commission marked the first time that an artist outside of the U.S. Mint had become involved in the production of an American coin. This coin and the Columbian quarter-dollar piece issued along with it also share the distinction of being the first American coins to feature portraits of historical figures.

83

As George Gurney has reconstructed it, the story of Warner's role in designing the Columbian half dollar illustrates the "fundamental difference in aesthetic approach" between the Mint engravers and the new generation of American sculptors trained in modeling, which caused increasing tension between the two groups. Because of a dispute between the Columbian Commission and the Mint over the portrait of Columbus that Warner had created for the coin, another portrait of the explorer, originally modeled by the sculptor for the medal commemorating the dedication of the Exposition (***83***), was adopted for the obverse of the half-dollar piece. A comparison of the obverses of the medal and the coin reveals the extent to which Mint engravers Charles E. Barber and George T. Morgan, who executed the dies for the coin from Warner's models, weakened the effect of the sculptor's subtle, plastic modeling. Having removed Warner's initials from the design, Barber and Morgan took full credit for the Columbian half dollar, and subsequent numismatic literature has omitted any mention of Warner as the designer of the coin, since his role in the project was not documented in Mint records.

Saint-Gaudens' design for the official award medal of the Columbian Exposition (***86***) also embroiled him in a controversy with the U.S. Mint

87

and officials of the Treasury Department. The sculptor's original design for the reverse of the medal, which featured an ideal nude youth representing the "Spirit of America," was rejected by the United States Senate Quadro-Centennial Committee because of the "impropriety" of the figure. When the Secretary of the Treasury requested that Saint-Gaudens redesign the piece, "covering the objectionable part of the figure," he initially refused to do so on aesthetic grounds. Eventually, however, he submitted two slightly modified versions of the reverse and a third version without the figure, but all three of these designs were rejected. Upon learning that the medal would be struck with a reverse by Mint engraver Charles E. Barber, adapted from his last design, Saint-Gaudens became incensed and took his case to the press, rallying his fellow artists to his defense.

While the nude figure in the initial version of the reverse of the Columbian award medal (*86*), modeled by Louis Saint-Gaudens, is somewhat awkwardly posed, the design is far superior to the banal reverse by Barber that was later struck (*87*). The contrast between the fluid, modeled surfaces of Saint-Gaudens' masterfully composed obverse and the precisely defined forms of Barber's busy reverse is immediately apparent. Among the many portrayals of Columbus on American and European medals commemorating the Exposition (**85**, **90**, and **91**, for example), Saint-Gaudens' obverse design stands out for its heroic treatment of the figure of the explorer, represented at the dramatic moment when he first stepped ashore in the New World. In comparison with Roty's delicate, allegorical design for the award medal of the French section of the Exposition (**88**), Saint-Gaudens' composition, with its vigorous naturalism, is closer in spirit to Quattrocento medals.

BIBLIOGRAPHY: John H. Dryfhout, *The Work of Augustus Saint-Gaudens* (Hanover, NH, and London, 1982), pp. 201-2, no. 151; Nathan N. Eglit, *Columbiana: The Medallic History of Christopher Columbus and the Columbian Exposition of 1893* (Chicago, 1965); MFA 1986, pp. 229-31; George Gurney, "Olin Levi Warner (1844-1896): A Catalogue Raisonné of His Sculpture and Graphic Work," Ph.D. diss., University of Delaware, 1978, vol. 1, pp. 177-80, vol. 3, pp. 766-94; William S. Nawrocki, "The Great Columbian Exposition," *Coinage* 18 (1982), pp. 32-33, 35-36, 40, 44; "New Columbus Medals," *AJN* 27 (1892/3), pp. 41-43; Homer Saint-Gaudens, ed., *The Reminiscences of Augustus Saint-Gaudens* (New York, 1913), vol. 2, pp. 45, 66-72; Malcolm Storer, "Medals of Columbus," *The Numismatist* 38 (1925), pp. 133-34, 197-99, 251-53, 315-17, 357-59, 406-8 and supplementary list by Robert P. King, *The Numismatist* 50 (1937), pp. 291-93, 396-97, 495-96, 600; Vermeule, pp. 91-96.

82. Columbian Exposition Commemorative Half Dollar, 1892 and 1893

Olin Levi Warner

Struck silver (U.S. Mint), 30 mm

Gift of Daniel Parish, Jr.

"The Columbian Half Dollar," *AJN* 27 (1892/3), p. 65; Craven, p. 409; Eglit 30; Gurney, vol. 1, pp.

177-80, vol. 3, 766-92; Taft, p. 275; Don Taxay, *An Illustrated History of U.S. Commemorative Coinage* (New York, 1967), pp. 3-8; Vermeule, pp. 91-92

83. **Director's Badge and Dedication Medal, 1892**
World's Columbian Commission
Olin Levi Warner
Struck: bronze, 34 mm; silver, 34 mm

Badge, gift of Stuyvesant Fisk
Eglit 334, 406; Gurney, vol. 3, pp. 793-94; Storer 135

84. Designers' Medal, 1892
Elihu Vedder
Struck bronze (Whiting Mfg. Co., N.Y.), 63 mm

Eglit 336; Storer 137

85. Christopher Columbus, 1893
American Numismatic Society
James H. Whitehouse
Struck bronze (Tiffany & Co.), 76 mm

AJN 28 (1893/4), pp. 53-54, 79; ANS History, p. 127; Belden, pp. 28-29; Eglit 104; Storer 1

86. **Award Medal, 1893**
Designed by Augustus Saint-Gaudens, modeled by Louis Saint-Gaudens
Proof cast with rejected reverse, bronze with painted modifications, 100 mm

AJN 28 (1893/4), pp, 58, 76; Dryfhout 1982, no. 151; IECM, p. 335, no. 27; MFA 1986, pp. 229-31; *Reminiscences*, vol. 2, pp. 45, 66-72; Vermeule, pp. 93-96

87. **Award Medal, 1894**
Obverse by Augustus Saint-Gaudens, reverse by Charles E. Barber
Struck (U.S. Mint): bronze, 76 mm; bronze with gilt obverse, silvered reverse, 76 mm

Gift of James D. McGuire and bequest of Dr. George F. Kunz
"The Columbian Exposition Medal," *AJN* 30 (1895/6), pp. 119-20; Eglit 90; IECM, p. 335, no. 23; Storer 160; Vermeule, pp. 93-96

88. French Section Award, 1894
Louis Oscar Roty
Struck (Paris Mint), silvered bronze, 50 x 53 mm

Eidlitz bequest and gift of Georges Roty
Dompierre de Chaufepié, p. 79; Eglit 234; IECM, p. 269, no. 28; Mazerolle 59

89. Commemorative Medal, 1893
Struck bronze (Lauer, Nuremburg), 114 mm

Eglit 338; Storer 150

90. Cristoforo Colombo, 1892
Modeled by Ludovico Pogliaghi, dies prepared by A. Cappuccio
Struck bronze (Stefano Johnson, Milan), 100 mm and 59 mm

AJN 27 (1892/3), p. 41; Eglit 106, 107; IECM, p. 251, no. 2; Storer 190, 191

91. Commemorative Medal, 1892/3
Struck aluminum (Orsini & Millefiori Inc., Rome), 90 mm

Eglit 102; Storer 9

Cotton States and International Exposition, Atlanta, 1895

The award medal of the 1895 Atlanta Exposition (***92***) is worthy of note as the sole work of medallic art by Philip Martiny (1858-1927), the talented architectural sculptor from Strasbourg who "brought the full range of ornamental work of the Beaux-Arts style to America" (Craven). After he came to this country in the 1880s, Martiny worked with Saint-Gaudens, for whom he modeled the George Washington centennial medal (***77***), and he had a major hand in the sculptural decorations for the World's Columbian Exposition. With its exuberant allegorical design and lively modeling, Martiny's Cotton States Exposition medal exemplifies the high Beaux-Arts style of decorative sculpture.

BIBLIOGRAPHY: Craven, pp. 473-75; NSS 1923, p. 259; Taft, pp. 452-56.

92

92. **Award Medal, 1895**
Philip Martiny
Struck: bronze, 57 mm; gilt bronze, 57 mm

Gift of the heirs of Dr. James Douglas and bequest of Dr. George F. Kunz

The Universal Expositions, Paris 1878, 1889, 1900

The official medals for the Universal Expositions held in Paris in 1878, 1889 and 1900 are important as precedents for the American Exposition medals. As Mark Jones has shown, the earliest of these pieces, Chaplain's medal for the 1878 Exposition (**93**), was innovative in its rejection of "the convention of a composition in fairly high relief which rises abruptly from a completely flat and polished field." The format of a pair of allegorical figures hovering above a bird's eye view of the Fair was repeated by Bottée in his medal for the 1889 Exposition (**94**) and again by Chaplain in his elegant design for the award medal of the 1900 Exposition (***95***). The American medalist Victor D. Brenner also created a commemorative badge for the 1900 Exposition (**97**), the first of the Paris Fairs at which the United States was significantly represented. A comparison of the refined pictorial compositions on the tiny piece by Brenner, which illustrate the American Pavilion at the Exposition and a monument to Lafayette given by the American people to the French, with the allegorical images on Roty's small commemorative plaquette for the 1900 World's Fair (**96**) reveals Brenner's stylistic debt to his teacher.

93. 1878 Paris Exposition Award Medal, 1879
Jules-Clément Chaplain
Struck silver, 67 mm

J. Coolidge Hills collection bequest
Jones, p. 120; Mazerolle 17

94. 1889 Paris Exposition Award Medal, 1889
Louis-Alexandre Bottée
Struck (Paris Mint): silvered bronze, 63 mm; bronze, 63 mm

Silvered bronze, bequest of Dr. George F. Kunz
AJN 28 (1893/4), pp. 58-59; IECM, p. 17, no. 15

95. **1900 Paris Exposition Award Medal, 1900**
Jules-Clément Chaplain
Struck (Paris Mint): bronze, 64 mm; silver, 64 mm

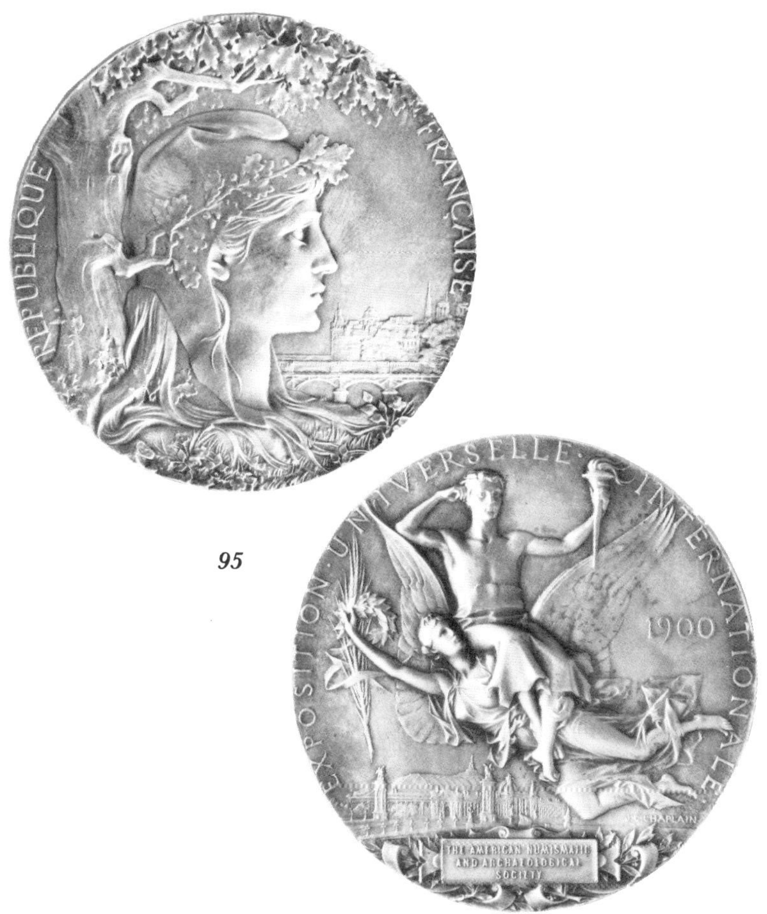

95

Dompierre de Chaufepié, p. 86; Mazerolle 132

96. 1900 Paris Exposition Commemorative Medal, 1900
Louis Oscar Roty
Struck (Paris Mint), silvered bronze, 50 x 35 mm

Dompierre de Chaufepié, p. 79; IECM, p. 269, no. 30; Mazerolle 173

97. American Pavilion, 1900 Paris Exposition, 1900
Victor D. Brenner
Struck badge (Paris Mint): gilt bronze, 45 x 29 mm; silver, 45 x 29 mm

Silver, gift of David R. Lit from the collection of Victor D. Brenner and bequest of Dr. George F. Kunz
G. Fuld, "Medallic Memorials to Lafayette," *The Numismatist* 70 (1957), pp. 1065-66, LA.1900.2; IECM, p. 29, no. 61; Smedley 33

98. 1900 Paris Exposition Commemorative Plaquette, 1900
Société des Amis de la Médaille Française
J. Edouard Roiné
Struck bronze (Paris Mint), 55 x 68 mm

Gift of Daniel M. Friedenberg
Dompierre de Chaufepié, p. 109; IECM, p. 263, no. 9, and p. 310, no. 31

The Hudson-Fulton Celebration, New York, 1909

The 1909 Hudson-Fulton Celebration, like the World's Fairs of 1893, 1901, 1904, and 1915, was an occasion for celebrating the achievements of America. Two weeks of naval parades, historical pageants, aquatic sports, aeronautical exhibitions, and pyrotechnics, among other events, celebrated the three-hundredth anniversary of Henry Hudson's discovery of the Hudson River in 1609 and the one-hundredth anniversary of Robert Fulton's first use of steam to navigate the same river in 1807. A huge outpouring of medals and tokens in all shapes and sizes accompanied the festivities held in New York City and the towns along the Hudson River. Medals for the Hudson-Fulton Celebration were commissioned from a number of the leading medallic sculptors of the day, including Chester Beach (***100***), John Flanagan (**101**), Emil Fuchs (*99*), and J. Edouard Roiné (**102**). It is interesting to note that Fuchs and Roiné were among the European immigrants who transmitted the continental style of medallic art to this country, while Flanagan and Beach were American sculptors trained in Paris.

99

The American Numismatic Society's Committee on the Publication of Medals made preliminary studies in the spring of 1908 for a medal commemorating the Hudson-Fulton Celebration and selected Emil Fuchs to design and model the piece according to their specifications. In an effort to make the details of the design as historically accurate as possible, the ANS Committee examined historical navigational tools, consulted authorities in various fields, and sent Fuchs to Holland to research Henry Hudson and Dutch ships of the early seventeenth century. Upon completion, the models for the medal were submitted to the Medal Committee of the Hudson-Fulton Commission, which decided to issue the piece jointly with the ANS as the official medal of the Celebration. A total of 124,698 examples of the medal (***99***), in a variety of sizes and metals, were struck before the dies were retired, making this one of the largest issues of a single medal ever produced.

According to Edward D. Adams, a member of both the ANS Medals Committee and the Hudson-Fulton Medal Committee, Fuchs introduced a deliberate contrast in the designs for the two sides of the medal. The reverse "was treated in a classical manner befitting the education and character of the engineer [Fulton], while the other side was given an aspect of dramatic action, as appropriate to the daring navigator and discoverer [Hudson] whose career ended in a tragedy of mutiny and mysterious death." Fuchs' distinctive soft style unifies the lively vignette of Henry Hudson and his sailors on the obverse of the medal and the calm, symmetrically balanced allegory of steam navigation on the reverse. Summarizing the merits of the piece, Adams wrote that this medal, with "the accuracy of its historical detail, the balance and grace of its composition, and the delicate refinement of its low relief," set a standard for the level of medallic and numismatic art that the ANS wished to foster.

None of the other medals for the Hudson-Fulton Celebration equals Fuchs' work in artistic quality or intricacy of design. For the obverse of the Official Badge, sanctioned by the Committee on Badges, Flags and Poster of the Hudson-Fulton Commission (***100***), Chester Beach employed the simple formula of jugate bust portraits of Henry Hudson and Robert Fulton. His design for the reverse features an allegorical figure representing the "Spirit of Progress," based on the central figure in the Official Poster for the Celebration, with the New York City skyline as a backdrop. Beach, like Fuchs, shapes his figures in soft, low relief, but his modeling is less varied. John Flanagan's design for the Hudson-Fulton medal issued by the Circle of Friends of the Medallion (**101**) is also disappointing, especially in contrast to the originality of many of his other medallic compositions. Jugate busts of Hudson and Fulton again comprise the obverse of the medal, while the reverse is occupied by a draped female figure who holds a light bulb, symbolizing the age of electricity, with the Hudson River and the skyline of New York in the background.

BIBLIOGRAPHY: Edward D. Adams, "Hudson-Fulton Medal," *AJN* 43 (1908/9), pp. 149-54; *The Hudson-Fulton Celebration, 1909*, Fourth Annual Report of the Hudson-Fulton Celebration Commission to the Legislature of the State of New York, 2 vols. (New York, 1910).

***99.* Official Commemorative Medal, 1909**
American Numismatic Society and Hudson-Fulton Celebration Commission
Emil Fuchs
Galvanos of obverse and reverse, copper, 330 mm; struck (Whitehead & Hoag Co.): bronze, 103 mm; silver, 76 mm

AJN 43 (1908/9), pp. 77-78, 149-54; ANS History, pp. 177-81; Belden, pp. 50-51; *Hudson-Fulton Celebration*, vol. 1, pp. 75-84, 517; IECM, p. 106, no. 14; *The Numismatist* 22 (1909), pp. 271-72

***100.* Commission Badge and Medal, 1909**
Chester Beach
Struck (Tiffany & Co.): silver badge, 38 mm; gold medal, 77 mm

Gold, Eidlitz bequest
Hudson-Fulton Celebration, vol. 1, pp. 39-40, 84-86, 523, 525; IECM, p. 8, no. 3

101. Commemorative Medal, 1909
Circle of Friends of the Medallion
John Flanagan
Struck bronze (Medallic Art Co.), 69 mm

Gift of Daniel M. Friedenberg
Chamberlain, p. 128; IECM, p. 92, no. 4

102. Souvenir Badge, 1909
Roiné and Weil
Cast bronze models of obverse and reverse (uniface), 204 x 141 mm; struck badge (Whitehead & Hoag Co.), aluminum, 38 x 26 mm

100

Models, gift of Mrs. George M. Hamilton in memory of Col. George M. Hamilton

103. Newburgh Hudson-Fulton Medal, 1909
Henry Kirke Bush-Brown
Struck bronze (Whitehead & Hoag Co.), 50 mm

Bequest of Dr. George F. Kunz
AJN 44 (1910), pp. 23-24; IECM, p. 37, no. 1

104. Hendrik Hudson Daalder, 1909
Designed by Frank C. Higgins, modeled by J. Edouard Roiné, issued by Thomas L. Elder
Cast bronze model of reverse, uniface, 199 mm; struck (Medallic Art Co.): silver, 38 mm; aluminum, 38 mm; bronze, 15 mm

Model, gift of Elliott Smith; silver, bequest of E. T. Newell; aluminum, gift of Ira, Lawrence and Mark Goldberg
Hibler and Kappen 369, 370, 373

105. Robert Fulton Dollar, 1909
Designed by Frank C. Higgins, modeled by J.

Edouard Roiné, issued by Thomas L. Elder
Cast bronze model of reverse, 199 mm; struck (Medallic Art Co.): gold, 15 mm; bronze, 15 mm

Model, gift of Elliott Smith
Hibler and Kappen 375, 377

The Pan-American Exposition, Buffalo, 1901

The award medal created by Hermon MacNeil for the 1901 Pan-American Exposition (***106***) is notable for its inventiveness. It is clear that the sculptor intended to produce a design that would be unmistakably American, as he stated at the time. While the motif of a woman with a butting animal featured on the obverse of the Pan-American medal goes back to Greco-Roman sources, as Cornelius Vermeule has noted, MacNeil recasts the female figure as a powerful nude, embodying the concept of Liberty, and the animal as a buffalo, a symbol both of America and of the city hosting the Exposition. His innovative composition for the reverse of this medal uses the image of a North American and a South American Indian sharing a peace pipe to symbolize Pan-American friendship. This geographical allegory would serve as an important model for subsequent American medals and coins.

Another noteworthy medal associated with the Pan-American Exposition is the special medal designed by James Earle Fraser in honor of Augustus Saint-Gaudens (***107***). The Saint-Gaudens medal, with its obvious borrowings from Quattrocento and classical sources, makes an instructive comparison with MacNeil's medal for the Buffalo Exposition. There is nothing in Fraser's design that marks it as specifically American, although his naturalistic treatment of the portrait of Saint-Gaudens is somewhat comparable to MacNeil's handling of the Indian figures on the reverse of his Pan-American medal.

106. **Award Medal, 1901**
Hermon MacNeil
Struck (Gorham & Co.): gilt bronze, 64 mm; bronze, 64 mm

Gift of Mrs. George M. Hamilton in memory of Col. George M. Hamilton and National Numismatic Collection (Museum of American History, Smithsonian Institution)
Craven, p. 519; W. T. R. Marvin, "The Pan-American Medal," *AJN* 36 (1901/2), pp. 40-42; NSS 1923, pp. 301, 359; Vermeule, pp. 131-32

107. **Special Medal of Honor for Augustus Saint-Gaudens, 1901**
James Earle Fraser
Struck bronze, 91 mm

The Metropolitan Museum of Art, 09.114 B (gift of Mr. and Mrs. Frederick S. Wait, 1909)
"The Special Medal of Honor Created for Augustus Saint-Gaudens," *The Century Magazine* 75 (1908), pp. 713-14; Craven, p. 492; Gardner, p. 128; NSS 1923, p. 355; Vermeule, p. 127

The Louisiana Purchase Exposition, St. Louis, 1904

For the Louisiana Purchase Exposition of 1904, Adolph A. Weinman created a unique series of medals (**108**, ***109***, **110-11**) struck in varying metals and shapes, depending on the class of the award. All of these medals share the same central obverse and reverse designs, set off by circular fields, but the motifs around the edges of the different pieces vary. On the obverse, the central medallion features an image of Liberty cloaking herself and a younger figure beside her in the American flag, an important precedent for Weinman's "Walking Liberty" half

107

dollar (*197*). The corresponding field on the reverse is filled by an American eagle with outstretched wings framing a cartouche for the inscription, with a pair of opposed dolphins flanking a scallop shell below. The smooth surfaces and elegant linear outlines which complement these restrained compositions are typical of the sculptor's style. A brief comparison of Weinman's medals for the St. Louis Fair with an elaborate plaquette by Bottée for the French section of the Exposition (**112**) underscores the clarity and balance of Weinman's designs.

BIBLIOGRAPHY: Kurt Krueger, *Meet Me in St. Louie: The Exonumia of the 1904 World's Fair* (Iola, Wisc., 1979).

108. Commemorative and Gold Medals, 1904
Adolph A. Weinman
Triangular, struck: bronze, 70 x 70 mm; gold, 70 x 70 mm
Gift of F. W. Clark and bequest of Dr. George F. Kunz
Krueger 16 and 20; Noe, pp. 22-23

***109.* Grand Prize Medal, 1904**
Adolph A. Weinman
Shield-shaped, struck gold, 73 x 64 mm
Bequest of Dr. George F. Kunz
Krueger 18; Noe, pp. 24-25

110. Silver Medal, 1904
Adolph A. Weinman
Replica, square, struck bronze, 67 x 67 mm
Krueger 14; Noe, pp. 26-27

111. Bronze Medal, 1904
Adolph A. Weinman
Struck bronze, 63 mm
Gift of Robert A. Weinman from the collection of Adolph A. Weinman
Krueger 12; Noe, p. 26

112. French Industrial Section, 1904
Louis Alexandre Bottée
Struck bronze (Paris Mint), 72 x 62 mm
Private collection, Brooklyn, New York
IECM, p. 17, no. 18

The Panama-Pacific Exposition San Francisco, 1915

Confronted with the problem of representing the opening of the Panama Canal on the official medals for the 1915 Panama-Pacific Exposition (**113** and **114**), the San Francisco trained sculptor Robert Aitken (1878-1949) and John Flanagan both turned to standard allegorical compositions. The reverse of Aitken's commemorative medal and the obverse of Flanagan's award medal for the San Francisco Exposition are similar in their use of a pair of nude figures to symbolize the uniting of Atlantic and Pacific, but Flanagan's vigorous, athletic nudes contrast sharply with Aitken's wispy, refined figures. Flanagan's skillful rendering of the Jewel Tower, the architectural centerpiece of the Fair, on the reverse of his medal, is unusual for an official American medal.

113. Official Commemorative Medal, 1915
Robert Aitken
Struck: silver, 38 mm; bronze, 38 mm
Gift of Farran Zerbe
AJN 49 (1915), pp. 201-2; Hibler and Kappen, 399, 400; *The Numismatist* 28 (1915), p. 143

114. Award Medal, 1915
John Flanagan
Struck: gilt bronze (Tiffany & Co.), 71 mm; bronze (U.S. Mint), 71 mm
Bequest of Dr. George F. Kunz and National Numismatic Collection (Museum of American History, Smithsonian Institution)
AJN 49 (1915), pp. 200, 203; *The Numismatist* 29 (1916), p. 169

109

The Flowering of Medallic Art

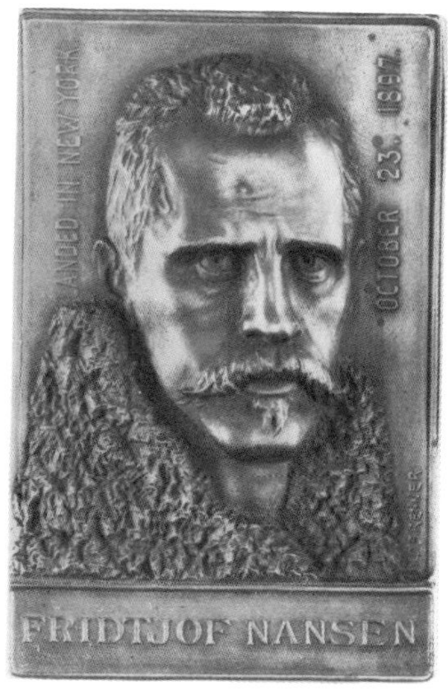

117

Victor David Brenner (1871-1924)

Victor David Brenner was born in Shavly, Lithuania in 1871. As a youth, he learned the engraving trade from his father, and he worked as a jewelry engraver and seal cutter in Russia before immigrating to New York in 1890. Within a few years he had established himself as a die cutter and engraver working for jewelers and silversmiths in New York. Brenner began his formal art studies in night classes at the National Academy of Design in 1896, and in 1898 he left for Paris for three years of further study. In Paris, he studied modeling at the Académie Julian and medallic art with Charpentier and Roty, in whose studio he worked also as an assistant.

Unlike many of the other American artists represented in this exhibition, whose medallic work was supplemental to major sculptural commissions, Brenner was a professional medalist. In fact, only a few works of sculpture by him are known. His choice of studying with Roty, the premier French medalist of the day, rather than entering the sculpture course at the Ecole des Beaux-Arts is significant in this respect. On his return to New York from Paris in 1901, Brenner was hired to teach a new course in coin and medal design jointly sponsored by the ANS and the National Academy of Design. Although he resigned from teaching after one year, he continued to promote the cause of medallic art with great zeal throughout his career. He was an active member of the ANS and published a brief pamphlet entitled *The Art of the Medal*, in which he described the various historical methods of medal production.

Brenner's earliest medals executed in New York before his departure for Paris already reveal his admiration for the contemporary French school of medalists. Two medals issued by the ANS, the Muhlenberg medal of 1896 (**116**) and the Charities and Corrections medal of 1898 (***118***) show a combination of the traditional hand engraving and modern reducing machine techniques of die cutting. The obverse of the Charities and Corrections medal features an attempt to render a group of classically inspired allegorical figures in the soft, decorative Parisian manner, but the composition is routine and the figures somewhat stiff and awkward. By contrast, Brenner's mastery as a portraitist is apparent even before his first trip to Paris, particularly in his 1897 plaquette (***117***) honoring Danish explorer Fridtjof Nansen. The force of personality and feeling of three-dimensional presence conveyed in this small piece are remarkable. With its daring frontal gaze, strong contrasts of light and shadow produced by the variation of the depth of relief, and dramatic sense of texture, the portrait of Nansen is a tour-de-force.

Portraiture continued to be the focus of Brenner's work during his Paris years. His plaquettes and medals from this period, represented here by the portraits of George Aloysius Lucas (***119***), Anita Stuart (**120**) and J. Sanford Saltus (**121**), show the direct influence of Roty's soft, painterly style. Light flickers across the surface of the extremely low relief, fusing figure and background in a delicate tonal study. Brenner's frequent choice of the plaquette format and his use of decorative foliage in these portrait compositions also show his debt to Roty.

While he continued to work in the manner of Roty, many of Brenner's portrait medals from the period after his return to America evidence a renewed interest in the naturalistic portrayal of his subjects. As always, Brenner is at his best as a portraitist, while the reverse designs for his medals are generally somewhat weak and highly derivative of Roty, with certain notable exceptions (***127*** and ***137***, for example). His finest portraits from this period, such as those of James McNeill Whistler (***127***), sculpted on a return trip to Paris, and Senator William Maxwell Evarts (**122**), combine a strong characterization of the individual, akin to the earlier Nansen portrait, with the pictorial concerns of the

Beaux-Arts style. In comparison with the Lucas portrait of 1899, the low relief modeling of the Whistler and Evarts portraits is more varied, giving the figures a greater sense of plasticity. The commemorative portrait of Whistler is particularly convincing, brilliantly evoking the cocky personality of the artist through the jaunty pose of the figure, the lively surface modeling, and the analogy with the splendid peacock which mirrors the figure of the artist on the reverse. The culmination of Brenner's medallic portraiture came a few years later with his famous portrait of Abraham Lincoln (**136** and ***137***), which has graced the obverse of the U.S. one-cent piece since 1909 (***193***).

BIBLIOGRAPHY: Victor D. Brenner, *The Art of the Medal* (New York, 1910), rpt. in *The Numismatist* 95 (1982), pp. 2238-55; Charles H. Caffin, "Victor D. Brenner, Medallist," *The International Studio* 17 (1902), pp. xci-xciv; Elvira Clain-Stefanelli, "V. D. Brenner," *Medallic Sculpture* 1 (1985), pp. 3-8; Forrer, vol. 1, pp. 277-79, vol. 7, pp. 117-22; Kathryn Greenthal, "Victor David Brenner," pp. 329-35 in MFA 1986; Grolier Club, *Catalogue of Medals and Plaques by Victor D. Brenner* (New York, 1907); IECM, pp. 26-34; Paul U. Kellogg, "Two New Worlds and a Sculptor's Clay," *The Survey* 35 (1915), pp. 19-22; Marx 1901, p. vii, pl. 29; NSS 1923, pp. 30, 274-75, 352; Glenn B. Smedley, "The Works of Victor D. Brenner: A Descriptive Listing," *The Numismatist* 96 (1983), pp. 1361-92, 1599-1606, and 97 (1984), pp. 2513-16; Vermeule, pp. 121-23; "Victor D. Brenner," *The Numismatist* 22 (1909), pp. 69-70; Whitney 1976, p. 262.

115. Dr. Chauncey M. Depew, undated
Struck: silver, 50 mm; pewter, 50 mm
Silver, Eidlitz bequest
Smedley 9; Stahl, p. 2068

116. William Augustus Muhlenberg, 1896
American Numismatic Society and St. Luke's Hospital
Struck: bronze, 50 mm; silver, 50 mm
Silver, gift of David R. Lit from the collection of Victor D. Brenner
AJN (1896/7), pp. 90-91; Belden, pp. 30-31; IECM 64; Smedley 19

***117.* Fridtjof Nansen, 1897**
Struck bronze (uniface), 69 x 45 mm
IECM 23; Smedley 20

***118.* Charities and Corrections Conference, New York, 1898**
American Numismatic Society
Struck: bronze, 76 mm; silver, 76 mm
Silver, gift of David R. Lit from the collection of Victor D. Brenner
ANS History, p. 131; Belden, pp. 34-35; IECM 9; Smedley 27

***119.* George Aloysius Lucas, Paris, 1899**
Cast bronze (uniface), 142 mm
Clain-Stefanelli, p. 3; IECM 25; MFA 1986, pp. 331-32, 110; Lillian C. Randall, ed., *The Diary of George A. Lucas: An American Art Agent in Paris, 1857-1909* (Princeton, 1979), vol. 1, p. 46, vol. 2, pp. 881-84; Smedley 28

120. Anita Stuart, Paris, 1899
Galvano, silvered copper, 108 x 91 mm
Museum of Fine Arts, Boston, 04.248 (gift of James Loeb)
Clain-Stefanelli, p. 3; IECM 5; MFA 1986, p. 332, 111; Smedley 32

121. J. Sanford Saltus, Paris, 1900
Galvano, silvered copper, 68 x 57 mm
Eidlitz bequest
IECM 34; Smedley 34

118

119

122. William Maxwell Evarts, 1902
Cast bronze (uniface), 157 x 119 mm; struck silver, 60 x 45 mm

Bronze, the Metropolitan Museum of Art, 07.125.10 (anonymous gift, 1907)
IECM 66; Smedley 42

123. Prince Henry of Prussia, 1902
American Numismatic Society
Struck: silver, 70 mm; bronze, 70 mm

AJN 36 (1901/2), p. 105; ANS History, p. 132; Belden, pp. 38-39; IECM 63; Smedley 43

124. Lloyd McKim Garrison Award, 1903
Harvard University
Struck bronze, 52 x 61 mm

Clain-Stefanelli, p. 4; IECM 38; Smedley 52

***125.* Amerigo Vespucci, 1903**
American Numismatic Society
Struck: gold, 58 x 77 mm; silver, 58 x 77 mm

Gift of Harry W. Bass, Jr., ex J. P. Morgan collection and Eidlitz bequest
ANS History, p. 143; Belden, pp. 40-41; Clain-Stefanelli, p. 4; IECM 4; Smedley 51

126. Collis Potter Huntington, 1904
Galvano, gilt bronze, 120 x 98 mm

Clain-Stefanelli, p. 5; IECM 11; Smedley 57

***127.* James McNeill Whistler, 1905**
Struck bronze (Paris Mint), 65 x 90 mm; galvano of reverse, silvered copper, 65 x 90 mm

Bronze, Eidlitz bequest; galvano, the Metropolitan Museum of Art, 06.293.2 (gift of Mr. and Mrs. Frederick S. Wait, 1906)
Clain-Stefanelli, p. 5; IECM 28; Smedley 62

128. John Paul Jones, 1906
American Numismatic Society
Struck (Paris Mint): silver, 60 x 80 mm; bronze, 60 x 80 mm

AJN 41 (1906/7), pp. 46-47; ANS History, pp. 171-73; Belden, pp. 42-43; Clain-Stefanelli, p. 5; IECM 32; Smedley 67

129. Spencer Trask, 1907
Struck silver, 83 x 90 mm

IECM 57 (variant); Smedley 75

130. Katrina Trask, 1907
Struck silver, 83 x 90 mm

IECM 36; Smedley 76

131. Yaddo, 1907
Reverse of Spencer (**129**) and Katrina (**130**) Trask plaquettes
Struck bronze (uniface), 82 x 89 mm

Gift of David R. Lit from the collection of Victor D. Brenner

132. J. Sanford Saltus Award, 1907
National Academy of Design
Struck bronze, 51 mm

IECM 45; Smedley 78

133. Panama Canal Service Medal, 1908
Struck bronze, 31 mm

National Numismatic Collection (Museum of American History, Smithsonian Institution)
Clain-Stefanelli, p. 7; IECM 48; *The Numismatist* 22 (1909), p. 71; Smedley 80; Todd Wheatley, "The Panama Canal Service Medal," *The Medal Collector* 34 (1983), pp. 4-17

134. Wright Brothers, 1908
Aero Club of America
Struck (U.S. Mint): silver, 76 mm; bronze, 76 mm

138

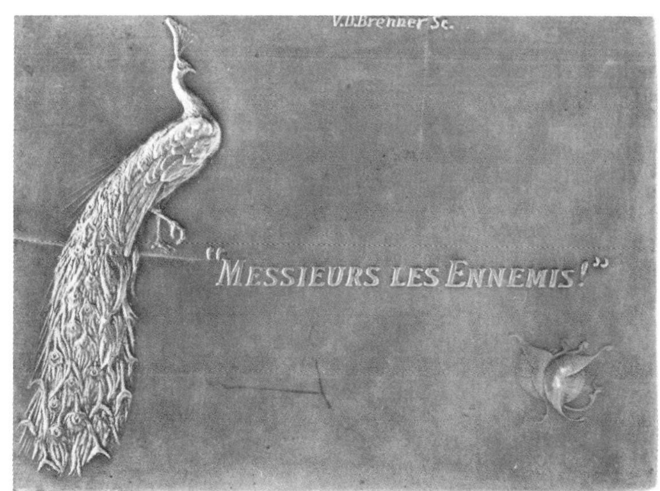

127

Clain-Stefanelli, p. 7; IECM 65; *The Numismatist* 22 (1909), p. 134; Smedley 81

135. American Numismatic Society, 1908
50th Anniversary Membership Pin
Struck silver (Tiffany & Co.), 24 mm

ANS History, p. 175; Belden, pp. 48-49; Smedley 82

136. Abraham Lincoln Centennial Plaquette, 1909
Struck bronze (uniface), 89 x 67 mm

Eidlitz bequest
Clain-Stefanelli, p. 7; IECM 2; Smedley 83; Vermeule, p. 122

***137.* Abraham Lincoln Centennial Medal, 1909**
Struck (Gorham & Co.): bronze, 63 mm; silver, 63 mm

AJN 43 (1908/9), pp. 22-23; Clain-Stefanelli, p. 8; IECM 1; King 304; *The Numismatist* 22 (1909), p. 40; Smedley 84

***138.* Norman Wait Harris Prize, 1909**
The Art Institute of Chicago
Struck bronze, 70 mm

Eidlitz bequest
IECM 6; Smedley 86

139. Joaquin Sorolla y Bastida, 1910
The Hispanic Society of America
Cast bronze, 89 mm

Clain-Stefanelli, p. 8; IECM 30; Smedley 91

140. Motherhood, 1911
Circle of Friends of the Medallion
Struck bronze (Jos. K. Davison's Sons), 70 mm

Chamberlain, p. 129; Clain-Stefanelli, p. 8; IECM 41; *The Numismatist* 26 (1930), p. 134; Smedley 87

141. Samuel Putnam Avery, 1914
Struck (Tiffany & Co.): bronze, 64 mm; silver, 64 mm

Eidlitz bequest
AJN 49 (1915), p. 203; NSS 1923, p. 352; Smedley 102

142. Warner & Swasey Co. Lick Telescope, 1920
Struck bronze, 77 mm; 1930 restrike (Medallic Art Co.), 63 mm

Clain-Stefanelli, p. 8; NSS 1923, p. 352; Smedley 117; Stahl, p. 2069

John Flanagan (1865-1952)

John Flanagan grew up in Newark, New Jersey, and began his art studies at the Cooper Union in New York City. He worked for a time as a modeler of architectural ornaments, and then entered the studio of Augustus Saint-Gaudens. During his three years as assistant to Saint-Gaudens, Flanagan continued his studies in night classes at the Art Students League. In 1890 he went to Paris, where he remained for twelve years, studying at the Académie Colarossi, at the Académie Julian with Chapu, and at the Ecole des Beaux-Arts in the atelier of Falguière. He also assisted Frederick MacMonnies in Paris with the colossal fountain group for the 1893 Columbian Exposition.

143

Although he sculpted a number of portrait busts and large-scale reliefs, Flanagan was chiefly a medalist throughout his career. One of his earliest surviving medallic portraits, the medallion of Mabel Clarke (***143***), executed in Paris between 1895 and 1898, is an elegant, masterful portrait in the Beaux-Arts tradition. The play of light across the softly modulated surface gives a sense of life to the figure, and the carefully rendered period details of her dress and hairstyle further the realistic impression of the piece. Like Saint-Gaudens, Flanagan incorporates the date and his monogram, with the trademark palmette motif, into the design of the medallion as a decorative feature, complemented here by a delicate rose which alludes to the woman's beauty.

After his return to America, Flanagan produced a series of distinctive portrait reliefs of literary figures and artist friends, employing both the medallion and plaquette formats. These portraits are again notable for the artist's skillful handling of light and shade, which conveys a sense of plasticity to the figures, despite the low relief. Flanagan's 1919 portrait of Walt Whitman (***156***), for example, with its strong modeling and the rippling lines of the hair and beard, gives a vivid impression of the poet's larger-than-life character. An earlier profile version of the Whitman portrait (**145**) in softer, lower relief is more meditative in tone, demonstrating Flanagan's facility at exploiting the technique of low relief modeling to achieve a wide range of effects.

Flanagan's commissioned medals are among the best American medallic work of this period. A number of his medals are particularly noteworthy for the realistic treatment of their subject matter. His 1915 award medal for the School Art League of New York City (***155***) depicts a female art student sketching from a model in the surroundings of a sculpture studio. A comparison with Chester Beach's medal for the Art Students League (***242***), which shows a lithe female figure holding a drawing pen and sketch pad in front of the New York City skyline, or James Earle Fraser's medals (***107***, **230**, and **234**) which represent the artist as a heroic male nude and Pegasus as a symbol of the Muses' inspiration, reveals the refreshing originality of Flanagan's design. The obverse of his medal for the Massachusetts Horticultural Society (***150***) and the reverse of his Essex Agricultural Society medal (***152***) likewise depict contemporary figures engaged in everyday gardening activities.

As Cornelius Vermeule has observed, other medals by Flanagan, such as the *Titanic* lifesaving medal (***154***), feature heroic Michelangelesque nudes, where a detailed, realistic presentation of the subject would be impossible in the space of the tondo. Flanagan's concern with the clarity of the image is evident also in his handling of inscriptions, which are kept simple and unobtrusive. The variety

150

154

of patinas used to color the surfaces of his reliefs and medals shows the artist's interest in the technical aspects of medallic production as well. His technical knowledge and skill earned him the praises of his contemporaries, including Frederick MacMonnies, who is reported to have said, "I consider him the leading medalist of America, an artist of high rank and a craftsman of infinite sincerity and devotion to his work."

BIBLIOGRAPHY: Forrer, vol. 2, p. 101, vol. 7, pp. 308-9, vol. 8, p. 347; Gardner, pp. 91-93; IECM, pp. 92-95; Marx 1901, p. vii, pl. 29; NSS 1923, pp. 63, 354-55; Frank Owen Payne, "John Flanagan—Sculptor and Medallist," *The International Studio* 75 (1922), pp. 114-16; Vermeule, pp. 124-26.

143. **Mabel Clarke, Paris, 1895-1898**
Galvano, gilt copper, 117 mm
IECM 6

144. Daniel Garrison Brinton, Paris, 1898
The Numismatic and Antiquarian Society of Philadelphia
Struck clichés of obverse and reverse, bronze, 64 mm

145. Walt Whitman, 1903
Cast bronze (uniface), 200 mm
Collection of the Newark Museum, 14.453

146. Leo Tolstoy, 1907
Galvano, bronze, 120 x 88 mm
IECM 5 (variant)

147. Aphrodite, 1908
Galvano, gilt copper, 116 mm
The Metropolitan Museum of Art, 09.38.5 (Rogers Fund, 1909)
Gardner, p. 92; IECM 2

148. Portrait of a Man, 1908
Wax model, 130 x 90 mm; negative galvano, copper, 156 x 116 mm; positive galvano, copper, 130 x 92 mm; cast bronze (uniface), 92 x 63 mm
Model and galvanos, collection of the Newark Museum, 27.775 A, B, and C
IECM 8

149. Horace Howard Furness Award, 1909
The Pennsylvania Society
Struck clichés of obverse and reverse, bronze, 70 mm
IECM 9

150. **George Robert White Medal of Honor, 1910**
Massachusetts Horticultural Society
Struck bronze, 70 mm
Eidlitz bequest
Vermeule, pp. 125-26

156

155

151. Ethel, New York, 1911
Cast bronze (uniface), 120 mm

***152.* Essex Agricultural Society of Massachusetts, 1913**
Struck clichés of obverse and reverse, bronze, 70 mm
AJN 47 (1913), pp. 148, 151; NSS 1923, p. 355

153. The Delver, 1913
Cast bronze (uniface), 151 mm
Collection of the Newark Museum, 14.454

***154.* Captain Arthur Henry Rostron, 1913**
Congressional Medal of Honor for the Rescue of Survivors of the *Titanic*
Struck clichés of obverse and reverse, bronze, 70 mm
Collection of the Newark Museum, 13.119 and 13.120
AJN 47 (1913), pp. 148, 151; NSS 1923, p. 355; *The Numismatist* 26 (1913), p. 265; Vermeule, p. 124

***155.* School Art League of New York City Award, 1915**
Struck bronze (Medallic Art Co.), uniface, 71 mm
Eidlitz bequest
AJN 49 (1915), p. 204; NSS 1923, p. 354

***156.* Walt Whitman, 1916-1919**
Cast bronze (uniface), 200 mm
NSS 1923, p. 355; *The Numismatist* 34 (1921), pp. 344-45

157. Daniel Chester French, 1919
Cast bronze (uniface), 140 x 99 mm
Gift of Robert A. Weinman from the collection of Adolph A. Weinman
NSS 1923, p. 354

158. Walter Griffin, Painter, 1919
Cast bronze (uniface), 118 mm
Gift of Robert A. Weinman from the collection of Adolph A. Weinman
NSS 1923, p. 354

159. Joseph Pennell, 1919
Cast bronze (uniface), 119 mm
NSS 1923, p. 354

160. Edward, Prince of Wales, 1919
American Numismatic Society
Struck: bronze, 63 mm; silver, 63 mm
Bronze, gift of Daniel M. Friedenberg
ANS History, pp. 120-21; NSS 1923, p. 354; *The Numismatist* 32 (1919), pp. 503-4

161. Garden Club of America Medal of Honor, 1920
Struck clichés of obverse and reverse, bronze, 70 mm
NSS 1923, p. 354; *The Numismatist* 34 (1921), pp. 344-45

162. Frederick William MacMonnies, 1929
Cast bronze (uniface), 150 x 115 mm
Collection of the Newark Museum, 29.801

163. Aphrodite/Swift Runners, 1932
Society of Medalists
Cast bronze (Medallic Art Co.), 73 mm

164. Augustus Saint-Gaudens, 1934
Cast bronze (uniface), 151 x 114 mm; struck bronze (Medallic Art Co., 1937), 63 x 46 mm
Cast bronze, collection of the Newark Museum, 35.20; struck bronze, gift of Robert A. Weinman from the collection of Adolph A. Weinman

Adolph Alexander Weinman (1870-1952)

Adolph Alexander Weinman was born in Karlsruhe, Germany, in 1870. He came to the United States with his family in 1880 and was apprenticed to a wood and ivory carver in New York at age fifteen. The following year he began studying

165

drawing and modeling in evening classes at the Cooper Union, and in 1890 he became an assistant to the sculptor Philip Martiny, a former pupil and assistant of Saint-Gaudens. While working with Martiny, Weinman continued his studies at the Art Students League under Saint-Gaudens. In 1895, after a brief period as assistant to Olin Levi Warner, Weinman entered Saint-Gaudens' studio, where he worked for several years. He subsequently assisted Charles Niehaus and Daniel Chester French, before setting up his own studio in 1904.

The exhibition of European medals at the World's Columbian Exposition in Chicago first brought this medium to Weinman's attention, and his interest in medallic art was undoubtedly furthered by his work with Warner and Saint-Gaudens. An early medallic portrait of his mother (***165***), dating from 1895, is closely comparable to Roty's own portrait of his mother on a plaque of his parents (***28***) executed in 1886. In contrast to Roty's precise, realistic rendering of the wrinkles and hollows of his aging mother's face, however, Weinman's treatment of his mother's features is softer and more generalized.

In his mature medallic work, Weinman moves further away from Roty's pictorialism, favoring instead a more severe, classicizing style, employed also in the architectural relief sculptures for which he is best known. His compositions focus in general on bold figural groups, with little, if any, background detail. His designs for the medals of the American Institute of Architects (***174***) and the National Institute of Arts and Letters (***176***), for example, feature classical themes—the Greek artists Polygnotos, Ictinos, and Pheidias appear on the AIA medal and the god Apollo on the NIAL medal—in simple, powerfully delineated compositions.

Studies from Weinman's collection which came to the ANS after his death show his method of working out the design for a medal. For the United States Medal for Lifesaving on Railroads, Weinman began with a two-figure composition (***172***) showing a rescue in action, but later reduced the design to a single nude figure symbolizing railroad heroism (***173***), more appropriate to the scale of the piece. In the simplified version, there is still a sense of urgent drama, conveyed primarily by the diagonal posture of the figure and the swirling linear movement of the composition, which beautifully complements the circular shape of the medal. Weinman's mastery of medallic composition and the balance of linear pattern and sculptural form in his work are epitomized in his design for the U.S. "Walking Liberty" half dollar (***197***), where he once again uses the elegant, sweeping curves of the drapery folds to create a sense of flowing movement.

BIBLIOGRAPHY: "Adolph Alexander Weinman," *Pan-American Union Bulletin* 45 (1917), pp. 775-87; "The Designers of the New Silver Coinage," *AJN* 49 (1915), pp. 210-12; Charles H. Dorr, "A Sculptor of Monumental Architecture," *Architectural Record* 33 (1913), pp. 518-32; Forrer, vol. 6, pp. 427-28, vol. 8, pp. 266-70;

172

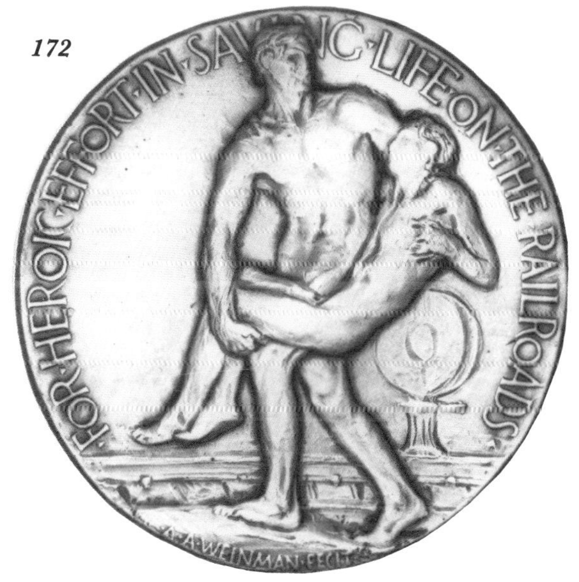

Gardner, p. 107; IECM, pp. 357-58; NSS 1923, pp. 246, 318-19, 362-63; Sydney P. Noe, *The Medallic Work of A. A. Weinman,* ANSNNM 7 (New York, 1921); NSS 1923, pp. 246, 318-19, 362-63; Vermeule, pp. 142-48; Robert A. Weinman, "Adolph A. Weinman," *National Sculpture Review* 1965/6, pp. 22, 28; Whitney 1976, p. 319.

174

165. **Catharina Weinman, 1896**
Galvano, silver, 90 mm
Gift of Robert A. Weinman
IECM 1; Noe, pp. 10-11

166. Alice Helen Hettinger, 1898
Galvano, gilt copper, 77 mm
Gift of Robert A. Weinman
Noe, p. 47

167. Louise Hettinger Medallion, 1900
Galvano, silver, 79 mm
Gift of Robert A. Weinman
Noe, p. 47

168. Louise Hettinger Plaque, 1900
Cast bronze (uniface), 226 x 134 mm
Gift of Robert A. Weinman
Noe, p. 47; NSS 1923, p. 362

169. Charles Yoce Harvey, 1902
Galvano, silver, 82 x 93 mm
Gift of Robert A. Weinman
Noe, pp. 14-15

170. The Rockinghorse Baby, 1902
Galvano, gilt copper, 79 mm
Noe, pp. 16-17

171. Bobbie, undated
Galvano, gilt copper, 85 mm

172. **For Heroic Effort in Saving Life on the Railroads, undated**
(Sketch for the U.S. Lifesaving Medal)
Galvano, gilt copper, 98 mm
Gift of Robert A. Weinman

173. **The United States Medal for Life Saving on Railroads, 1906**
Struck: gilt bronze, 43 mm; bronze, 44 mm; galvano, gilt copper, 77 mm
Galvano, gift of Robert A. Weinman
IECM 3; Noe, pp. 18-21; NSS 1923, p. 363

173

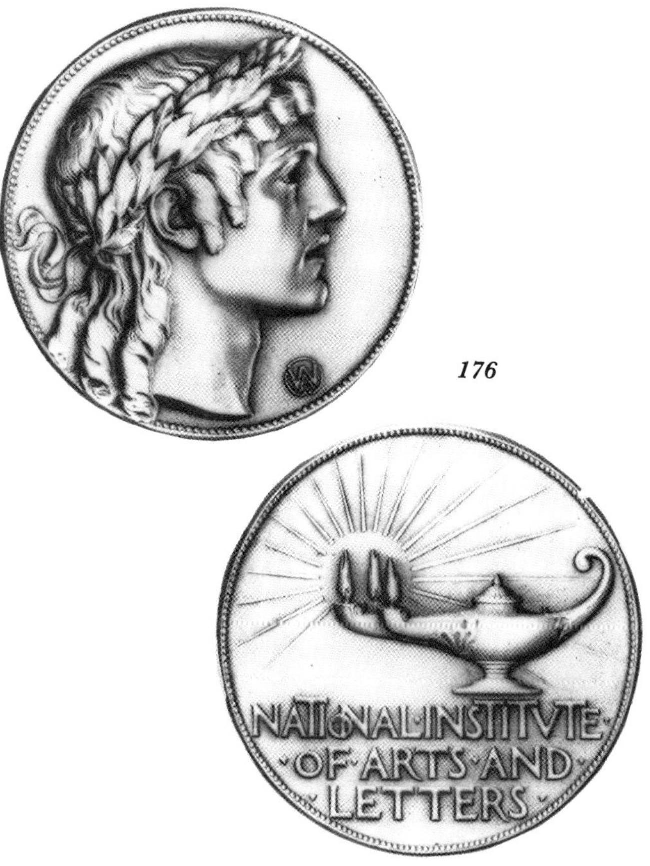

176

***174.* American Institute of Architects, 1907**
Struck: bronze, 56 mm; cliché of reverse, gilt bronze, 56 mm

Cliché, gift of Robert A. Weinman
Noe, pp. 30-31

175. The Edison Medal, undated
(Sketch for a competition)
Galvano, gilt copper, 77 mm

Gift of Robert A. Weinman
Noe, p. 47; NSS 1923, p. 363

***176.* National Institute of Arts and Letters, 1909**
Struck bronze, 58 mm; cast of reverse (uniface), gilt bronze, 58 mm

Cast, gift of Robert A. Weinman
Noe, pp. 32-33

177. The Charge, 1909
Cast bronze (uniface), 126 x 169 mm

Gift of Robert A. Weinman
IECM 4

178. Naval Battle, undated
Cast bronze (uniface), 128 x 167 mm

Gift of Robert A. Weinman

179. G. M. S[tark]., 1910
Galvano, gilt copper, 128 x 62 mm

Gift of Robert A. Weinman
Noe, p. 47; NSS 1923, p. 362

180. Katherine Jane Weinman, 1915
Galvano, gilt copper, 98 mm

Noe, pp. 36-37; NSS 1923, p. 362

181. United States Navy Dominican Campaign Medal, 1916
Struck: bronze, 33 mm; cliché of reverse, gilt bronze, 38 mm

Cliché, gift of Robert A. Weinman

***182.* J. Sanford Saltus Award, 1919**
American Numismatic Society
Galvano, gilt copper, 450 mm; struck silver, 79 mm

ANS History, p. 214; Noe, pp. 44-46; NSS 1923, pp. 319, 362-63; Vermeule, p. 144

183. Julius Theodore Melchers, Sculptor, undated
Galvano, gilt copper, 108 mm

Gift of Robert A. Weinman
Noe, p. 47

184. Theodore Vail Public Service Medal of A.T.& T., 1922
Struck: bronze (Medallic Art Co.), 64 mm; cliché of obverse, bronze, 64 mm

Cliché, gift of Robert A. Weinman
NSS 1923, pp. 362-63; *The Numismatist* 35 (1922), p. 234

Janet Scudder (1873-1940)

Janet Scudder grew up in Terre Haute, Indiana, and first studied sculpture with Louis Rebisso at the Cincinnati Art Academy. In 1891 she moved to Chicago, where she worked briefly as a wood carver and then became one of Lorado Taft's assistants on the sculptures for the World's Columbian Exposition. When the Exposition ended, she went to Paris to study with Frederick MacMonnies, whose Columbian fountain she had particularly admired. In Paris, she studied at the Académies Vitti and Colarossi before being admitted to MacMonnies' studio as a pupil and assistant. She returned to New York for a short time in 1896, securing enough commissions to go back to Paris and set up her own studio. A trip to Italy led her to produce the first of the charming Renaissance-inspired fountain sculptures which were to become her specialty. She lived near Paris for many years, making periodic trips to New York to exhibit and market her works.

Like many of her contemporaries, Scudder supplemented her income in the early years of her career with commissions for portrait plaquettes and medallions. Her accomplished low relief portraits, with their wealth of decorative detail, beautifully capture the elegant world of her cosmopolitan patrons. Of particular interest are the elaborate decorative frames which she incorporates into the compositions of her portrait plaquettes, such as those of Arthur Middleton Reeves (***187***) and a Woman with a Japanese Fan (***191***). The Reeves portrait, illustrated here in an untrimmed cast, is almost overwhelmed by its fanciful medievalizing frame. An exquisitely detailed period frame, draped with tassels, complements the portrait of a fashionable woman holding a Japanese fan, a sign of her refined taste.

BIBLIOGRAPHY: Forrer, vol. 5, pp. 447-50; Gardner, pp. 114-15; Hill 1984, pp. 13-14, 49; IECM, pp. 301-3; Rena Tucker Kohlman, "America's Women Sculptors," *The International Studio* 76 (1922), pp. 225-26; Leila Mechlin, "Janet Scudder—Sculptor," *The International Studio* 39 (1910), pp. lxxxi-lxxxviii; NSS 1923, p. 224; Janet Scudder, *Modeling My Life* (New York, 1925).

185. Alice Jones, Paris, 1900
Cast bronze (uniface), 108 x 59 mm
IECM 2

186. Bishop Hare, 1904
Cast bronze (uniface), 109 x 92 mm
IECM 3; Mechlin, p. lxxxviii

***187.* Arthur Middleton Reeves, 1904**
Cast bronze (uniface, untrimmed), 122 x 94 mm

188. Master Billy Fahnestock, 1904
Cast bronze (uniface), 157 mm
Hill 1984, p. 49, no. 34; IECM 9; Mechlin, p. lxxxviii

189. Alice, 1906
Galvano, silver, 112 x 90 mm
The Metropolitan Museum of Art, 06.1331.2 (Rogers Fund, 1906)
Gardner, p. 115; IECM 1

190. Mildred Barnes, 1906
Galvano, silvered copper, 110 x 97 mm
IECM 10

***191.* Woman with a Japanese Fan, undated**
Galvano, silvered copper, 128 x 92 mm

192. Indiana Centennial Medal, 1916
Struck bronze (Medallic Art Co.), 63 mm; struck bronze, 38 mm
Gift of J. Sanford Saltus and gift of William O. Marx
The Numismatist 29 (1916), p. 543

187

The U.S. Mint and Beaux-Arts

201

200

The Redesign of the Coinage

A century ago, James Kimball, director of the United States Mint, complained that the nation's coinage was inferior in design "to the same kind of work by almost every other advanced nation of the earth." Our coins, he added, were "keenly felt by many as unworthy of the development which the arts of sculpture and design here have attained." In 1891, fortified with Congressional sanction to change any coin design in use for twenty-five years or more, the Treasury organized a public competition for appropriate new designs. The result was by all accounts a fiasco: the jury found none of the 300 proposals suitable for adoption, and only two were deemed worthy of honorable mention. The mint director was unwilling to concede defeat, however, for "the money of a nation is expressive of its art culture....Lest posterity imagine the present generation to have been barbarous, it is desirable that our silver pieces should be as handsome as may be." Though he recognized French coinage as the best currently produced, Kimball sought to avoid "foreign" designs by entrusting the renovation of the U.S. coinage to the British-born chief engraver of the Mint, Charles E. Barber.

Barber's designs for the 1892 dime, quarter, and half dollar were competent but almost identical to each other, and they were judged visually unexciting. Two years later, the National Sculpture Society admonished the Secretary of the Treasury to "consider the unsatisfactory coinage of the United States....The whole body of our numismatic art compares badly with that of any one of the great nations of Europe." Not only would artistic coins support "the nation's claim to be a cultivated and enlightened one," but they would also afford regular lessons in artistic design "for the more discriminating members of the populace." Soon the American Numismatic Society joined with the Sculpture Society, as did six additional prestigious organizations, in the battle for new coin designs.

Neither public outcry nor organized lobbying, however, was sufficient to effect the desired changes. Skilled sculptors with a shared sensibility, a vital advance in technology, and political initiative at the highest level—all would contribute to the issue of the most artistically successful series of coins in this country's history. By 1900 the Beaux-Arts aesthetic had profoundly shaped a generation of sculptors and medalists, foremost among whom was Augustus Saint-Gaudens. The Janvier reducing lathe had made it possible for relief sculptors to create coin images without special training in die sinking. And then there was President Theodore Roosevelt.

Roosevelt had shown his distaste for the style prevailing at the U.S. Mint by designating Saint-Gaudens to sculpt a special medal for his second inaugural (***78***). Not only did the president admire the result, he found a kindred soul in Saint-Gaudens and entrusted to him the project of redesigning the country's circulating coinage. There followed an informal personal correspondence, in which Roosevelt joked that his actions could lead to impeachment or fatalities among the Mint staff, and Saint-Gaudens responded that if the mortality rate rose there, it would at least be for a good cause. Roosevelt suggested that even if impractical for modern needs, the high relief characteristic of the gold coins of Alexander the Great might serve as an ideal for the new issues. Sculptor and president agreed that a compromise—lower than ancient relief and raised rims to allow stacking—would be necessary to "avoid too heavy an outbreak in the mercantile classes." The president's suggestions for design elements were also heard sympathetically: the Ptolemaic eagle on his inaugural medal would appear not only on the reverse of Saint-Gaudens's ten-dollar gold piece (***201***), but also on the Pratt five-dollar and two-and-a-half-dollar gold pieces (***200*** and ***199***), as well as on de Francisci's 1921 silver Peace Dollar (**198**). Even Roosevelt's idea that an

Indian war bonnet should replace Liberty's traditional Phrygian cap was adopted for the ten-dollar coin. This indigenous headdress has often been seen as an incongruous addition to the classical profile of Liberty, derived from the Victory on Saint-Gaudens's Sherman monument and ultimately from Hellenistic sculpture.

The story of how the 1907 Saint-Gaudens double eagle, or twenty-dollar gold piece, was issued in the face of determined opposition from Chief Engraver Barber has been the subject of several detailed accounts. With its obverse of a striding Victory, again related to the Sherman monument, and its flying eagle reverse (adapted from an earlier U.S. one-cent piece), the original high relief version of the coin (***202***) is generally acknowledged to be the finest numismatic issue in U.S. history. By contrast, the "business strike" issues of 1907 through 1933 (***203***) with their low relief, arabic numerals, and "In God We Trust," suffer from the weakening of the coin's design imposed by Barber's machinations, "mercantile concerns," and Congressional piety. Yet even the faded glory of these regular issues sets standards seldom approached by other coins of the modern era.

Saint-Gaudens' death in late 1907 did not deter Roosevelt from his renovation of the coinage. Early in 1908, the President's friend Dr. W. S. Bigelow suggested that a new design for the fractional gold coinage be modeled in incuse rather than in the usual raised relief. He recommended Bela Lyon Pratt, a former student of Saint-Gaudens, for the job. With Roosevelt's enthusiastic approval of the models, and despite some inevitable tampering by Barber, the new half eagle (***200***) and quarter eagle (**199**) were issued with no advance public notice. Essentially identical, these coins carry on their reverse an intaglio version of Saint-Gaudens' standing eagle. The obverses feature the head of a rugged Indian chief in war bonnet. Symbolic representations of the New World and Liberty had long utilized Native Americans, but usually in an idealized manner. Pratt's naturalistic treatment of the Indian marked an important advance in the presentation of authentic Americana on the nation's coinage.

Before he left office in 1909, Roosevelt effected the redesign of the one-cent piece, a commission Saint-Gaudens had been unable to complete before his death. While the president was posing for the Panama Canal Service Medal (**133**), Victor Brenner offered to prepare a coin design featuring a portrait of Lincoln. The idea of portraying a real person, especially a president, instead of ideal types on a circulating coin must have been particularly appealing to Roosevelt. The centenary of Lincoln's birth was at hand, and Brenner had ready for inspection the model of the Lincoln plaquette (**136**) he had just completed. Daily familiarity with the U.S. cent's current appearance makes it difficult for us to appreciate Brenner's subtle and effective modeling (***193***). His early training as a die engraver enabled him to add to the master die details which contribute to the impressionistic play of light on Lincoln's hair, cheekbone, and beard.

The momentum for the redesign of the coinage built up in Roosevelt's second term carried into the administrations of Taft and Wilson. The five-cent piece was the only coin eligible for retirement under the twenty-five year rule when new designs were solicited in 1911. The commission again went outside the Mint, to James Earle Fraser, a French trained sculptor who had worked with Saint-Gaudens. Fraser's "buffalo" or "Indian head" nickel (***194***) represents the high point of the use of indigenous themes, handled in a realistic manner, in American coin design. The "buffalo," actually a bison, was modeled from life (albeit in a New York zoo), and the Indian was a composite portrait drawn from three members of different tribes. The bison's hump and lowered head are configured to the round of the tondo, as are the individual feathers at the back of the Indian's head. The powerful simplicity of the obverse is enhanced by the small numerals and lettering and by the omission of the usual invocation of the Deity. Later issues slightly modified the exergue of the reverse, but the coin retained its artistic integrity to its final year of issue in 1938.

193 194 196

In 1916 the Barber dime, quarter, and half dollar reached the end of their twenty-five year mandate. Working closely with the Commission of Fine Arts, the Mint invited a large number of prominent artists, including Barber and his assistant George Morgan, to submit sketches for new designs. The Commission supported Treasury Secretary MacAdoo's decision to award contracts for the dime and half dollar to Adolph A. Weinman and for the quarter to Hermon MacNeil.

The designs of Weinman, who was trained by Saint-Gaudens and influenced by Roty, exemplify the adaptation of the Beaux-Arts style to United States coinage. The obverse Liberty with winged cap—misidentified as Mercury by much of the public—and the fasces on the reverse of his dime (**195**) have been seen as containing specific references to France, the object of much American concern in 1916. Weinman's half dollar (***197***) conveys a similar message in larger format. The "Walking Liberty" of the obverse recalls Roty's "Semeuse" or "Sower" design on the French two-franc piece, but she is wrapped in an American flag; the reverse features a standing eagle, similar to the noble birds of Saint-Gaudens.

Hermon MacNeil's "Liberty Standing" quarter of 1916 (***196***) also reflects a mood favoring American intervention in the World War on behalf of France. MacNeil's design for the obverse of the quarter is based on the obverse of Brenner's 1909 medal for the Chicago Art Institute (***138***), which had in turn been modeled on similar compositions by Roty. The palette and brushes of Brenner's female personification have been replaced with patriotic iconography, and the classical parapet is now decorated with thirteen stars and bears the motto "In God We Trust." Liberty's militant stance is somewhat balanced by the olive branches in her right hand and the soft draperies which leave her right breast exposed. In 1917, as the nation prepared for war, Secretary MacAdoo insisted that this Liberty be girded with chain mail, concealing the breast that had sparked public outcry.

Today, sentiment has been voiced for a redesign of our circulating coinage. To find sculptors of the calibre of those who reshaped the American coinage between 1907 and 1921 will, indeed, be a major challenge.

William L. Bischoff
Assistant Curator of Modern Coins
The American Numismatic Society

BIBLIOGRAPHY: American Numismatic Society, Minutes of Special Meeting, Feb. 5, 1894; "Concerning the Eagles," *AJN* 42 (1907/8), pp. 41-47; John H. Dryfhout, *The 1907 United States Gold Coinage* (Cornish, N.H., 1972), and *The Work of Augustus Saint-Gaudens* (Hanover, N.H. and London, 1982), pp. 280-87; Willard B. Gatewood, "Theodore Roosevelt and the Coinage Controversy," *American Quarterly* 18 (1966), pp. 35-51; Kathryn Greenthal, *Augustus Saint-Gaudens, Master Sculptor* (New York, 1985), pp. 164-66; Henry Hering, "History of the $10 and $20 Gold Coins of 1907 Issue," *The Numismatist* 52 (1949), pp. 455-58; "The New Designs for Our Coinage," *AJN* 26, (1891/2), pp. 1-3; "The New Gold Coinage," *AJN* 42 (1907/8), pp. 36-40; "The Movement to Improve the Designs on Our Coinage," *AJN* 29 (1894/5), pp. 98-100; Homer Saint-Gaudens, ed., *The Reminiscences of Augustus Saint-Gaudens*, (New York, 1913), vol. 2, pp. 329-33, 336, 341, and "Roosevelt and Our Coin Designs," *The Century Magazine* 99 (1920), pp. 721-36; Don Taxay, *The U.S. Mint and Coinage: An Illustrated History from 1776 to the Present* (New York, 1966); Vermeule.

***193*. United States One-Cent Piece, type 1, 1909**
Victor D. Brenner
Struck copper

Taxay 1966, pp. 330-39; Vermeule, pp. 121-23

***194*. United States Five-Cent Piece, 1913**
James Earle Fraser
Struck nickel

Gift of Becky Adelson
AJN 47 (1913), p. 145; Taxay 1966, pp. 340-46; Vermeule, pp. 128-31

195. United States Dime, 1916 and 1917
Adolph A. Weinman
Struck silver

Gift of Howland Wood
NSS 1923, p. 363; Taxay 1966, pp. 347-53; Vermeule, pp. 145-46

***196*. United States Quarter Dollar, type 1, 1917, and type 2, 1917 and 1918**
Hermon MacNeil
Struck silver

Edward Groh Purchase Fund and gift of Howland Wood

197

NSS 1923, pp. 301, 359; Taxay 1966, pp. 347-53; Vermeule, pp. 139-42

197. **United States Half Dollar, 1916 and 1921**
Adolph A. Weinman
Struck silver

Edward Groh Purchase Fund
NSS 1923, p. 363; Taxay 1966, pp. 347-53; Vermeule, pp. 146-48

198. United States Silver Dollar, 1921 and 1923
Anthony de Francisci
Struck silver

Gift of Dr. George F. Kunz and gift of Robert L. and Marie Saxe
NSS 1923, pp. 279, 353; Taxay 1966, pp. 354-59; Vermeule, pp. 148-52

199. United States Two-and-a-Half-Dollar Gold Piece, 1908
Bela L. Pratt
Struck gold

Bequest of Arthur J. Fecht and gift of Richard H. Lawrence
Taxay 1966, pp. 325-29; Vermeule, pp. 119-21

200. **United States Five-Dollar Gold Piece, 1908 and 1909**
Bela L. Pratt
Struck gold

Bequest of Arthur J. Fecht
Taxay 1966, pp. 325-29; Vermeule, pp. 119-21

201. **United States Ten-Dollar Gold Piece, 1907**
Augustus Saint-Gaudens
Struck gold

Gift of J. P. Morgan and bequest of Arthur J. Fecht
Dryfhout 1972; Dryfhout 1982, pp. 281-82, no. 204-B; Greenthal 1985, pp. 164-66; Hering; Taxay 1966, pp. 308-25; Vermeule, pp. 111-19

202. **United States Twenty-Dollar Gold Piece, 1907**
Augustus Saint-Gaudens
Struck gold, high relief version

Bequest of Arthur J. Fecht
Dryfhout 1972; Dryfhout 1982, pp. 283-87, no. 204-C; Greenthal 1985, pp. 164-66; Hering; Taxay 1966, pp. 308-25; Vermeule, pp. 111-19

203. **United States Twenty-Dollar Gold Piece, 1907 and 1908**
Augustus Saint-Gaudens
Struck gold, business strikes

Gift of J. Sanford Saltus and bequest of Arthur J. Fecht
Dryfhout 1972; Dryfhout 1982, pp. 283-87, no. 204-C; Greenthal 1985, pp. 164-66; Hering; Taxay 1966, pp. 308-25; Vermeule, pp. 111-19

209

Medals by Charles E. Barber and George T. Morgan

By the turn of the century, Mint engraver Charles E. Barber and his assistant George T. Morgan (1845-1925) were producing medals in an updated, French inspired style. An Englishman like the Barbers, Morgan had studied at the Birmingham and South Kensington art schools and worked in London before immigrating to America in the 1870s. Appointed a "special engraver" by the U.S. Mint in 1876 to redesign the silver dollar, Morgan became assistant engraver in 1879 and chief engraver after Charles Barber's death in 1917.

A comparison of Barber's portrait of Benjamin Harrison for the 1889 inaugural medal (***65***) and his medallic portraits of Theodore Roosevelt (**206-208** and ***209***) evidences his change from working in high relief to modeling in the soft, low relief style developed in France. On the Roosevelt medals, thin, modern lettering replaces the heavy, Gothic inscriptions used for the Harrison medal. While Cornelius Vermeule has argued that Barber's portraits of Roosevelt, with their careful attention to the details of the president's attire and facial features, "perfectly, incisively characterize" the leader "whose watchword was action," Roosevelt himself was so displeased with the medal produced by Barber and Morgan for his second inauguration in 1905 (**207**) that he asked Augustus Saint-Gaudens to create an alternate inaugural medal (***78***). Saint-Gaudens' Roosevelt inaugural medal may be more aesthetically interesting than the official Mint medal, but the sculptor's idealized portrait of the president is less effective than Barber's straightforward bust.

Roosevelt had more reason to complain about a 1907 medal designed by Barber and Morgan to commemorate the departure of the U.S. Atlantic fleet from Hampton Roads (***209***). While the Hampton Roads medal is innovative for the Mint in its use of an irregular plaquette format, the obverse of this piece bears a portrait of Roosevelt only slightly varied from that which had appeared on official medals since his 1901 inauguration. Morgan's design for the reverse of the Hampton Roads medal closely recalls Chaplain's reverse for his 1893 medal commemorating the visit of the Russian fleet to Toulon (***11***). The similarity of the compositions and the nearly identical stance of the allegorical figure, who represents on the one hand Liberty or Columbia and on the other France, prove that the medal by Chaplain served as the direct model for Morgan's design. In comparison with Chaplain's restrained classicism, Morgan's trite handling of the figure and drapery and his addition of a superfluous cherub to the composition suggest that at least some of the criticisms of Barber and Morgan's medallic art were warranted.

BIBLIOGRAPHY: Forrer, vol. 4, p. 148, vol. 7, pp. 76-77 (George T. Morgan); IECM, pp. 334, 336-37; Francis Pessolano Filos, *The Assay Medals and the Assay Commissions, 1841-1977* (New York, 1983); "Report of the Committee on United States Medals," *AJN* 45 (1911), pp. 96-98; Vermeule, pp. 103-6, 108-9, 132-34.

204. Lifesaving Medal to Crew of the *Hudson*, 1900
By act of U.S. Congress for valour at Cardenas, May 1898
Struck bronze (U.S. Mint), 77 mm
National Numismatic Collection (Museum of American Art, Smithsonian Institution)
IECM, p. 334, no. 5

205. William McKinley Commemorative Medal, 1901
Obverse by Charles E. Barber, reverse by George T. Morgan
Struck bronze clichés of obverse and reverse (U.S. Mint), 77 mm
IECM, p. 334, no. 21; U.S. Mint 1972, no. 124; Vermeule, pp. 103-4

206. Annual Assay Medal, 1904
Struck (U.S. Mint): silver, 56 x 40 mm; bronze cliché of reverse, 56 x 40 mm
Silver, J. Coolidge Hills collection bequest
Assay Medals, p. 47, no. FMA-943; Vermeule, p. 104

207. Theodore Roosevelt Inaugural Medal, 1905
Obverse by Charles E. Barber, reverse by George T. Morgan
Struck bronze (Jos. K. Davison's Sons), 44 mm
AJN 39 (1904/5), p. 112; MacNeil, pp. 55-56

208. Theodore Roosevelt, 1905
Obverse by Charles E. Barber, reverse by George T. Morgan
Struck bronze (U.S. Mint), 75 mm
IECM, p. 334, no. 11; U.S. Mint 1972, no. 125; Vermeule, pp. 108-9

***209*. Theodore Roosevelt/Hampton Roads, 1907**
Obverse by Charles E. Barber, reverse by George T. Morgan
Struck bronze (U.S. Mint), 60 x 79 mm
AJN 45 (1911), pp. 96-97; IECM, p. 334, no. 7; U.S. Mint 1972, no. 532; Vermeule, pp. 108-9

210. William Howard Taft, 1909
Obverse by Charles E. Barber, reverse by George T. Morgan
Struck bronze (U.S. Mint), 76 mm
AJN 45 (1911), p. 96; IECM, p. 334, no. 13; U.S. Mint 1972, no. 126; Vermeule, pp. 132-4

211. Wilbur and Orville Wright, 1909
By act of U.S. Congress
Obverse by Charles E. Barber, reverse by George T. Morgan
Struck bronze and restrike (U.S. Mint), 56 x 81 mm
Restrike, gift of Michael Kirk
AJN 45 (1911), p. 97; IECM, p. 334, no. 19; *The Numismatist* 22 (1909), pp. 231-32

212. Annual Assay Medal, 1910
Struck bronze (U.S. Mint), 44 mm
J. Coolidge Hills collection bequest and gift of the Committee on U.S. Medals
AJN 44 (1910), pp. 131-32, and 45 (1911), pp. 97-98; *Assay Medals*, p. 55, no. FMA-949; Vermeule, pp. 132-34

The Legacy of Paris and Saint-Gaudens

213

Frederick William MacMonnies (1863-1937)

Frederick MacMonnies was born in Brooklyn and began his career as an apprentice in Saint-Gaudens' New York studio at the age of seventeen, studying drawing in night classes at the Cooper Union and National Academy of Design. At the encouragement of Saint-Gaudens, he went to Paris in 1884 for further studies, first at the Académie Colarossi and later at the Ecole des Beaux-Arts with Mercié and Falguière, who employed him as an assistant. By 1889 he had established his own studio in Paris, where he created his sensational centerpiece for the World's Columbian Exposition, the colossal fountain sculpture known as *The Barge of State* or *Triumph of Columbia*, which brought him instant fame. MacMonnies lived in France until 1915, when he returned to New York.

Although MacMonnies executed only a few medallic works, he merits consideration as the American sculptor who most thoroughly absorbed the decorative French style. Bemoaning the fact that the sculptor did not consider medallic art more worthy of his attention, the French critic Roger Marx remarked on the "originality" and "artistic excellence" of the few medals exhibited by MacMonnies at the 1900 Paris Exposition. His Niagara medal (***213***), engraved in Paris by Tasset, depicts an American Indian, a favorite subject of American sculptors at this time. In contrast to MacNeil's (***106***) or Fraser's (***194***) more closely observed Indian figures, MacMonnies' Indian is an elegant nude in the French tradition, set within a lively, decorative composition.

BIBLIOGRAPHY: Royal Cortissoz, "An American Sculptor: Frederick MacMonnies," *The Studio* 6 (1895), pp. 17-26; Craven, pp. 420-28; Edward J. Foote, "An Interview with Frederick W. MacMonnies, American Sculptor of the Beaux-Arts Era," *New York Historical Society Quarterly* 61 (1977), pp. 102-23; Forrer, vol. 3, p. 525, vol. 8, pp. 14-15; Gardner, pp. 82-85; IECM, pp. 199-200; Paula M. Kozol, "Frederick William MacMonnies," pp. 293-98 in MFA 1986; Will H. Low, "Frederick MacMonnies," *Scribner's Magazine*, 18 (1895), pp. 617-28; Marx 1901, p. vii, pl. 29; NSS 1923, p. 155; Taft, pp. 332-55; Whitney 1976, pp. 290-91.

213. **Niagara, undated**
Cataract Construction Company
Modeled by MacMonnies; engraved by Paulin Tasset
Struck (uniface), silvered bronze, 58 mm
Eidlitz bequest
IECM 1; Low, pp. 617-22

Helen Farnsworth Mears (1876-1916)

A native of Oshkosh, Wisconsin, Helen Farnsworth Mears studied briefly with Lorado Taft at the Art Institute of Chicago, executing her first major sculpture, *The Genius of Wisconsin*, for the 1893 Chicago World's Fair. In 1894 she went to New York to study with Saint-Gaudens at the Art Students League. She worked for a year as an assistant to Saint-Gaudens in New York and then traveled to Paris, where she studied under Charpentier, Collin, and Merson at the Académie Vitti and under Puech at the Académie Julian. She also assisted Saint-Gaudens in his Paris studio after his return from New York in 1897.

Mears' portrait plaque of Saint-Gaudens (**214**), dated Paris, 1898, shows the sculptor pausing from his work on the Sherman monument, a model of which appears in the background. Like many of Saint-Gaudens' own portrait reliefs, this piece, with its lively, textured surface, has the feeling of a quick sketch, catching the subject in an intimate pose.

BIBLIOGRAPHY: Forrer, vol. 8, p. 42; Gardner, pp. 125-26; IECM, pp. 213-14.

214. Augustus Saint-Gaudens, Paris, 1898
Cast bronze (uniface), 190 x 217 mm
IECM 1

Bela Lyon Pratt (1867-1917)

Bela Lyon Pratt grew up in Norwich, Connecticut, and entered the Yale School of Fine Arts at the age of sixteen. In 1887 he went to New York to study at the Art Students League with Augustus Saint-Gaudens and the painters Kenyon Cox and William Merritt Chase. Pratt worked as an assistant in the Saint-Gaudens studio for a short time before going to Paris in 1890. In Paris he studied with Falguière at the Ecole des Beaux-Arts and worked also with Henri Chapu. After his return to the United States, he worked on the sculpture for the World's Columbian Exposition and moved to Boston, where he taught modeling for many years at the School of the Museum of Fine Arts.

Although Pratt's medals were only a very small part of his total sculptural output, his medallic work seems to have brought him great personal satisfaction. His granddaughter, Cynthia Kennedy Sam, who is preparing a monograph on the sculptor, notes that Pratt often sculpted his medals during vacations or in his spare time, sometimes sketching them in a "white heat" of creativity, in his own words. The creation of a medal to commemorate the bicentennial of his alma mater, Yale University (**217**), was for Pratt a special labor of love.

His Henry Wadsworth Longfellow medal for the Cambridge Historical Society (***218***) and his New Theatre medal for the ANS (***220***) illustrate an original feature of a number of Pratt's medals, the use of a foliate wreath to frame the composition. Not only does the carefully detailed border add decorative interest to the piece, but its repetition on both obverse and reverse unifies the two sides of the medal. The softly modeled head of Longfellow is very much in the Beaux-Arts tradition, while the medal commemorating the opening of the New Theatre in New York, with its highly decorative figural compositions and sinuous line, perfectly captures the spirit of the Gilded Age. This medal may in fact best be seen as a miniature version of Pratt's architectural reliefs, such as his medallions of the Seasons for the Library of Congress or his decorative friezes for the Boston Opera House, which are closely comparable in style. Interesting use is made of the ornamental wreath on the obverse of the New Theatre medal, where the sensuous nude figure holding a mirror rests her foot on the frame, as if she is about to stand up and step out of the picture.

BIBLIOGRAPHY: "Bela Lyon Pratt," *The Pan-American Union Bulletin* 44 (1917), pp. 66-76; Lorinda Munson Bryant, "Bela Lyon Pratt: An Appreciation," *The International Studio* 57 (1916), pp. cxxi-cxxv; Craven, pp. 495-97; Charles Henry Dorr, "Bela L. Pratt: An Eminent New England Sculptor," *Architectural Record* 35 (1914), pp. 509-18; William Howe Downes, "The Work of Bela L. Pratt, Sculptor," *The International Studio* 38 (1909), pp. iii-x; Forrer, vol. 4, p. 684, vol. 8, pp. 145, 357; Paula M. Kozol, "Bela Lyon Pratt," pp. 309-22 in MFA 1986; "Memorial Exhibition of the Work of Bela Lyon Pratt," *Bulletin of the Museum of Fine Arts, Boston* 16 (1918), pp. 28-29; Taft, pp. 491-96; Vermeule, pp. 119-21; Whitney 1976, pp. 298-99.

215. Elizabeth and Clara Shattuck, 1893
Galvano, silvered copper, 92 mm
Collection of Cynthia Kennedy Sam
Craven, p. 496

216. Charles William Eliot, 1894
25th Anniversary as President of Harvard University
Cast, gilt bronze, 98 mm; struck proof, lead, 96 mm
Cast, Museum of Fine Arts, Boston, 18.1 (gift of Dr. Charles W. Eliot)
MFA 1986, pp. 312-13, no. 101

217. Yale University Bicentennial, 1901
Struck silver (Tiffany & Co.), 69 mm
Gift of Harry A. Colgate
AJN 36 (1901), p. 65

***218.* Henry Wadsworth Longfellow Centennial, 1907**
Cambridge Historical Society
Struck bronze, 63 mm

218

220

219. Archbishop William O'Connell, 1908
Centennial of the Roman Catholic Diocese of Boston
Struck bronze, 75 mm

***220.* The New Theatre of New York, 1909**
American Numismatic Society
Struck (Medallic Art Co.): bronze, 104 mm; silver, 76 mm

ANS History, p. 183; Belden, pp. 56-57

Herbert Adams (1858-1945)

Herbert Adams was born in West Concord, Vermont, and studied at the Massachusetts Normal School of Art in Boston. From 1885 to 1890 he was in Paris, where he studied and worked as an assistant in the atelier of Mercié at the Ecole des Beaux-Arts. On his return to America, he taught for a number of years at the Pratt Institute in Brooklyn and established a studio in Cornish, New Hampshire. Best known for his softly carved marble busts of women, Adams also created delicate bas-relief portraits in marble and bronze (**221**), inspired by the portrait reliefs of his Cornish neighbor Augustus Saint-Gaudens. Later in his career he designed a number of medals which are unexceptional in design, but worthy of note for their refined low relief modeling.

BIBLIOGRAPHY: Craven, pp. 434-37; Forrer, vol. 8, p. 308; Gardner, pp. 66-68; "Herbert Adams," *The Pan-American Union Bulletin* 45 (1917), pp. 93-104; NSS 1923, pp. 2, 266-67, 351; Ernest Peixotto, "The Sculpture of Herbert Adams," *The American Magazine of Art* 12 (1921), pp. 151-59; Taft, pp. 385-93.

221. Peggy Gantt, Cornish, N.H., 1912
Cast (uniface), gilt bronze, 165 x 129 mm

NSS 1923, pp. 267, 351; Peixotto, p. 159

222. For Good Diction on the Stage, undated
American Academy of Arts and Letters
Struck (Medallic Art Co.), gilt bronze, 50 mm

Eidlitz bequest

223. Anton Henry Classen, 1922
Classen High School Medal of Honor
Struck bronze (Medallic Art Co.), 56 mm

Eidlitz bequest

224. Joseph Hodges Choate, 1922
American Numismatic Society and Century Association
Struck bronze (Medallic Art Co.), 63 mm

ANS History, p. 223; NSS 1923, pp. 266, 351; *The Numismatist* 35 (1922), p. 253

Frances Grimes (1869-1963)

Born in Braceville, Ohio, Frances Grimes studied with Herbert Adams at the Pratt Institute in Brooklyn and worked from 1894 until 1900 as his assistant in his Cornish, New Hampshire, studio. In 1900, she became an assistant in the neighboring

Saint-Gaudens studio, where she was employed until the sculptor's death in 1907.

Following the example of Adams and Saint-Gaudens, Grimes sculpted a number of portrait reliefs of Cornish neighbors and their children. Her charming portraits of children, for example the relief of Harold Tripp Clement (***225***), are very close to similar pieces by Adams in their soft modeling and use of a format derived from Saint-Gaudens in which a low parapet in the foreground defines the pictorial space. A more inventive work by Grimes is the beautiful decorative plaque of the goddess Diana (**226**), poetically inscribed in Greek. The lyrical nude figure in an imaginary landscape is close in spirit to late nineteenth-century French pieces of this type by followers of Roty.

BIBLIOGRAPHY: Forrer, vol. 7, p. 397, vol. 8, p. 350; Gardner, p. 105; IECM, pp. 118-19; NSS 1923, pp. 88, 294-95, 357.

225. **Harold Tripp Clement, Jr., 1921**
Galvano, gilt copper, 168 x 122 mm
NSS 1923, pp. 295, 357

226. Diana, undated
Cast bronze (uniface), 249 x 142 mm
Private Collection, Arlington, Virginia

225

Henry Hering (1874-1949)

A native New Yorker, Henry Hering studied at the Cooper Union and Art Students League. He also worked with the sculptor Philip Martiny in New York for six years before traveling to Paris for further study at the Académie Colarossi and the Ecole des Beaux-Arts. In 1900 Saint-Gaudens hired Hering as a studio assistant, and he worked at Cornish until the master's death in 1907.

Hering's most important contribution to American medallic art was his modeling of Saint-Gaudens' designs for the U.S. ten and twenty-dollar gold pieces, which he discussed in a 1949 article in *The Numismatist*. Due to Saint-Gaudens' illness, it was Hering who played the role of go-between in the dispute with the Mint over the striking of the coins. In the tradition of the "Saint-Gaudens School," he also produced some portrait plaques and medallions in low relief (**227** and **228**). With their clearly delineated forms and smooth surfaces, these portrait reliefs illustrate the relatively strong idealistic tendency of Hering's sculpture in comparison with the more naturalistic direction of work by other Saint-Gaudens students.

BIBLIOGRAPHY: Guy Pené du Bois, "The Works of Henry Hering," *Architectural Record* 32 (1912), pp. 510-29; Forrer, vol. 7, pp. 440-42; Henry Hering, "History of the $10 and $20 Gold Coins of 1907 Issue," *The Numismatist* 52 (1949), pp. 455-58; IECM, p. 131; NSS 1923, p. 101.

227. Alice Olin Dows and Stephen Olin Dows, 1909
Cast bronze (uniface), 142 mm
Du Bois, pp. 520, 522; IECM 1

228. Evarts Tracy, 1912
Cast bronze (uniface), 112 x 167 mm
Eidlitz bequest
Du Bois, pp. 520, 525; Eidlitz 1000

James Earle Fraser (1876-1953)

James Earle Fraser was born in Winona, Minnesota, and grew up in the frontier Dakota Territory. After high school he moved to Chicago and entered the studio of the sculptor Richard Bock. He studied at the Art Institute of Chicago for a short

229

time, and at age nineteen went to Paris, where he studied with Falguière at the Ecole des Beaux-Arts and also attended classes at the Académies Julian and Colarossi. Impressed with Fraser's work at the Paris Salon of 1898, Augustus Saint-Gaudens invited the younger sculptor to become one of his assistants. Fraser worked with Saint-Gaudens for two years in Paris and returned with him to America in 1900 to assist him in his New Hampshire studio. In 1902 Fraser established his own studio in New York City, and from 1906 until 1911 he taught at the Art Students League.

While Fraser was still working with Saint-Gaudens, he was invited by the commissioners of the Pan-American Exposition to create a special medal honoring the outstanding exhibition of works by his mentor at the Buffalo Exposition. Fraser's striking design for the obverse of the Saint-Gaudens medal (***107***), with its noble portrait bust of the sculptor, is based on the Quattrocentro composition used by Saint-Gaudens a few years earlier for his George Washington medal (***77***). The reverse of the Saint-Gaudens medal features a classicizing allegory of sculpture, represented by a heroic male nude holding a hammer and chisel and Pegasus, a symbol of the Muses' inspiration. The motif of the winged horse is repeated by Fraser in a number of his other medallic compositions, both for its symbolic value and for visual effect.

Fraser's debt to Saint-Gaudens is also apparent in his relief portraits, which met with great success. A portrait plaque of the children of Harry Payne Whitney on horseback (***229***) shares the delicate low relief modeling of Saint-Gaudens' portrait reliefs, but the gentle texturing of the surface and the early Renaissance restraint of the piece mark it as Fraser's work. His most famous portrait is that of Theodore Roosevelt, first sculpted as a bust in 1909/10 and later adapted for a cast relief (**238**) and the Medal of Honor of the Roosevelt Memorial Association (***237***). The forthright realism of Fraser's portrait of Roosevelt, which vividly captures his subject's personality, marks a departure from Saint-Gaudens' more idealized portrayal of the president (***78***), although the same Italian Renaissance models inform both artists' work.

Fraser's finest medal, the Harriman Memorial medal of the American Museum of Safety (***233***), illustrates his ability to blend successfully contemporary realism and Renaissance tradition. Once again he employs the Quattrocento format of a bust portrait surrounded by simple lettering for the obverse, while on the reverse he depicts a track walker in contemporary garb striding along the rails. The realism of this treatment of the theme of railroad safety contrasts sharply with Weinman's symbolic representation of the same subject on the U.S. Lifesaving medal (***173***). Fraser's textured modeling of the reverse of the Harriman medal, also used very effectively in his portraits of Roosevelt, adds to the vigour of the towering figure, which is barely contained within the space of the tondo.

BIBLIOGRAPHY: Craven, pp. 492-94; Forrer, vol. 7, pp. 319-21, vol. 8, p. 348; Gardner, pp. 127-28; "James Earle Fraser," *The Pan-American Union Bulletin* 46 (1918), pp. 648-55; Dean Krakel, *End of the Trail* (Norman, OK, 1973); Joseph F. Morris, ed., *James Earle Fraser* (Athens, GA, 1955); NSS 1923, pp. 66, 286-87, 355; Elizabeth Anna Semple, "James Earle Fraser, Sculptor," *The Century Magazine* 79 (1910), pp. 929-32; Vermeule, pp. 111, 127-31; Whitney 1976, pp. 272-73.

229. **Flora and Sonny-Boy Whitney, undated**
Cast bronze, 166 x 192 mm
Craven, p. 493; NSS 1923, p. 355

230. Sculpture, undated
(Sketch for the reverse of the Saint-Gaudens medal?)
Cast bronze, 152 mm

231. Thomas Alva Edison Award, 1909
American Institute of Electrical Engineers
Struck: bronze, 69 mm; gilt bronze, 69 mm
Eidlitz bequest and Conner-Rosenkranz, New York

237

232. Seated Nude Holding a Light Bulb, undated
(Sketch for the Edison medal?)
Cast bronze, 115 mm

233. **Edward H. Harriman Memorial Medal, 1914**
American Museum of Safety
Struck: silver (Medallic Art Co.), 70 mm; gilt bronze (Tiffany & Co.), 70 mm
Gift of Mrs. William Sproule and bequest of Dr. George F. Kunz
AJN 48 (1914), p. 211; NSS 1923, p. 355; Vermeule, p. 127

234. American Academy of Arts and Letters, 1915
Struck bronze (Medallic Art Co.), 70 mm
Eidlitz bequest
NSS 1923, p. 355

235. New York State Soldiers and Sailors Award (1898-1900), 1915
Struck bronze (Medallic Art Co.), 34 mm
AJN 49 (1915), p. 204

236. American Institute of Graphic Arts Award, 1920
Struck bronze (Medallic Art Co.), 70 mm
Eidlitz bequest and gift of Robert A. Weinman from the collection of Adolph A. Weinman
NSS 1923, p. 355

237. **Roosevelt Memorial Association, 1920**
Struck bronze (Medallic Art Co.), 82 mm; cast bronze (variant), 70 mm
Cast, bequest of Dr. George F. Kunz

238. Theodore Roosevelt, 1920
Cast bronze (Decorative Arts League), 324 x 252 mm

Chester Beach (1881-1956)

A native of San Francisco, Chester Beach studied architectural modeling at the Lick Polytechnic School and drawing at the Mark Hopkins Institute there before leaving for Paris in 1904. In Paris, he studied with the sculptors Verlet and Roland at the Académie Julian. Upon his return to America in 1907, he established a studio in New York, where he remained, with the exception of a year spent in Rome in 1911.

Beach's designs for the reverse of the official badge for the 1909 Hudson-Fulton Celebration (***100***) and his medal for the School Art League of New York (***242***) are very similar in conception, sharing the "low relief planes," the elegant female personifications, and "the love of geography and vistas"—here the dramatic backdrop of the Hudson River and the skyline of New York—characteristic of his art (Vermeule). With their wispy figures and sinuous line, his works evoke the spirit of turn-of-the-century Vienna, and he in fact employs decorative *art nouveau* letter forms, comparable to those used by Heinrich Kautsch (***266***). While it is true that Beach's style lends itself at times to affectation, as Vermeule contends, the best of his medals, such as the School Art League piece, are imaginative and charming.

BIBLIOGRAPHY: Forrer, vol. 7, p. 58, vol. 8, p. 310; Gardner, p. 141; IECM, pp. 8-9; NSS 1923, pp. 21,

242

270-71, 351; Beata Beach Porter, "Chester Beach," *National Sculpture Review* 14, no. 3 (1965). pp. 20, 24-25; Vermeule, pp. 165-67, 171, 174-75, 189-90.

239. Saint Nicholas Society Anniversary Dinner, 1909
Struck bronze (uniface), 77 x 55 mm
IECM 5

240. Actors' Fund Fair, New York, 1910
Struck bronze (Medallic Art Co.), 70 mm
Eidlitz bequest
IECM 1

241. Beal Medal, undated
American Gas Institute
Struck silver, 50 mm
IECM 2

***242*. Saint-Gaudens Medal for Draughtsmanship, 1917**
School Art League
Struck bronze (Medallic Art Co.), uniface, 63 mm
Eidlitz bequest
NSS 1923, pp. 270, 351; Vermeule, p. 166

243. Children's Year, 1918/19
Children's Bureau, U.S. Department of Labor and Woman's Committee Council of National Defense
Struck bronze (Medallic Art Co.), 52 mm
Eidlitz bequest
NSS 1923, pp. 270, 351; *The Numismatist* 32 (1919), pp. 217-18

Daniel Chester French (1850-1931)

Born in Exeter, New Hampshire, Daniel Chester French moved with his family to Concord, Massachusetts, at the age of seventeen. There he took his first art classes with Abigail May Alcott and taught himself modeling. In 1870 he worked for a short time with sculptor John Quincy Adams Ward in New York, and in 1871 and 1872 he studied, also briefly, with William Rimmer and William Morris Hunt in Boston. Two years later he left for Italy, where he worked in the Florence studio of expatriate sculptor Thomas Ball. After his return to America in 1876, French worked in both Washington and Boston as an architectural sculptor. In 1886 he went again to Europe, this time to Paris to perfect his modeling technique. On his return to the United States, he settled in New York, embarking on a long and extremely successful career, which brought him many honors.

Primarily known as a sculptor of ideal monuments, French created only a few medals, and most of these were executed late in his career, with the help of assistants. His finest medals were all produced in association with the American Numismatic Society (***245***, ***317***, and **327**), of which he was a member. The only cast medal ever issued by the ANS, French's 1917 medal commemorating the completion of the Catskill Aqueduct (***245***) shares the classical vocabulary and boldly defined, yet fluidly modeled, form of his monumental sculptures. The beautiful, ideal head and beaded border of the obverse of this medal recall the masterpieces of Greek numismatic art. An equally beautiful, lyrical head of Victory, modeled in more delicate, low relief, graces the obverse designed by French for the ANS medal commemorating the visit of the French and British War Commissions to New York in 1917 (***317***). The trench helmet with a sprig of oak, a lily, and a cluster of pine needles bound to it as emblems of England, France and the United States eloquently symbolizes the meeting of the Allies, which is represented also in allegorical form on the reverse created for this medal by sculptor Evelyn B. Longman (1874-1954), a former assistant in French's studio. Longman's design is executed in a more stylized, archaizing manner, befitting the medieval figures of Joan of Arc and a knight, who personify France and England seeking the aid of American Liberty.

BIBLIOGRAPHY: Adeline Adams, *Daniel Chester French, Sculptor* (Boston, 1932); Selwyn Brinton, "D. C. French," *The International Studio* 46 (1912), pp. 210-14, and "The Recent Sculpture of Daniel Chester French," *The International Studio* 59 (1916), pp. 17-24; Charles A. Caffin, "Daniel Chester French, Sculptor," *The International Studio* 20 (1903), pp. cxxxiii-vi; William A. Coffin, "The

245

Sculptor French," *The Century Magazine* 59 (1900), pp. 871-79; Craven, pp. 392-406; "Daniel Chester French," *The Pan-American Union Bulletin* 44 (1917), pp. 66-76; Forrer, vol. 2, pp. 155-56, vol. 7, p. 326, vol. 8, p. 349; Gardner, pp. 57-60; Paula M. Kozol, "Daniel Chester French," pp. 250-55 in MFA 1986; NSS 1923, pp. 70, 290-91, 356; Michael T. Richman, *Daniel Chester French: An American Sculptor* (New York, 1976); Edwin A. Rockwell, "Daniel Chester French," *The International Studio* 41 (1910), pp. lv-lxii; Lorado Taft, "Daniel Chester French, Sculptor," *Brush and Pencil* 5 (1900), pp. 145-63; Taft, pp. 310-31; Whitney 1976, pp. 273-74.

244. Commodore Dewey, 1898
Struck copper (Tiffany and Co.): trial strike, final proof strike, medal and badge, 46 mm
Trial strike and medal, gift of Dr. George F. Kunz; final proof strike, gift of William S. Dewey; badge, National Numismatic Collection (Museum of American History, Smithsonian Institution)
AJN 33 (1898/9), p. 129

***245*. Catskill Aqueduct, 1917**
American Numismatic Society
Cast bronze (Medallic Art Co.), 76 mm
Bequest of Dr. George F. Kunz
ANS History, pp. 216-17; NSS 1923, pp. 290, 356; *The Numismatist* 30 (1917), p. 511

246. Lafayette Memorial, Brooklyn, 1917
Anthony Lukeman, after Daniel Chester French
Struck bronze (Medallic Art Co.), 51 x 63 mm
Eidlitz bequest
Melvin and George Fuld, "Medallic Memorials to Lafayette," *The Numismatist* 70 (1957), p. 1067, LA.1917.2; NSS 1923, p. 356; *The Numismatist* 32 (1919), p. 133

247. Joseph Pulitzer Medal, undated
Columbia University
Struck bronze (Medallic Art Co.), 70 mm
Eidlitz bequest
NSS 1923, p. 356

John Gutzon de la Mothe Borglum (1867-1941)

The son of an immigrant Danish woodcarver, Gutzon Borglum was born near Bear Lake, Idaho, and grew up in Nebraska. He attended St. Mary's College near Topeka, Kansas, and then went in the early 1880s to Los Angeles, where he was apprenticed to a lithographer and fresco painter. Before going to Paris in 1890, he studied painting at the Mark Hopkins Art Institute in San Francisco. In Paris, he studied painting with Lefebvre and Constant and sculpture with Mercié at the Académie Julian. He was most impressed, however, by the sculpture of Rodin. After several periods of travel in Europe, Borglum established a studio in New York in 1902. His talent was quickly recognized when he exhibited at the St. Louis World's Fair in 1904, and, although he taught for a short time at the Art Students League in 1906-7, his life was soon consumed by the giant sculptural projects which he undertook at Stone Mountain and Mount Rushmore.

Best remembered for his carvings on mountains, the sculptor who felt that "only the colossal matched the spirit of the United States" nevertheless did not overlook the art of the medal.

Borglum's member's medal for the American Numismatic Society (***248***) makes an interesting comparison with French's Catskill Aqueduct medal (***245***). The realistic nude figure depicted on the obverse of the member's medal is in sharp contrast to the ideal, athletic youth represented on the reverse of the Catskill Aqueduct medal. Borglum's handling of the figure, who turns with ease in the shallow space established by the rim of the medal to give a view of the medallion which he holds out in front of him, is masterful. The combination of simple naturalism and bravura modeling in this piece is reminiscent of Charpentier, the French medalist strongly influenced by Rodin, whom Borglum is known to have admired. Even closer to certain works by Charpentier is the image on the obverse of Borglum's Livingstone Centenary Medal for the American Geographical Society (***251***), which shows a wraith-like female figure, the Genius of the mountains, swirling through a rocky gorge in a cloud of vapor. Only a few gouged lines aid in defining the forms that emerge from the freely modeled surface of the extremely low relief.

BIBLIOGRAPHY: Robert J. Casey and Mary Borglum, *Give the Man Room: The Story of Gutzon Borglum* (New York, 1952); Craven, pp. 488-92; Forrer, vol. 7, p. 97; Gardner, pp. 100-102; IECM, p. 15; "Gutzon Borglum," *The Pan-American Union Bulletin* 44 (1917), pp. 479-88; Leila Mechlin, "Gutzon Borglum, Painter and Sculptor," *The International Studio* 28 (1906), pp. xxxv-xliii; NSS 1923, p. 27; Howard and Audrey Karl Shaff, *Six Wars at a Time: The Life and Times of Gutzon Borglum* (Sioux Falls, SD, 1985); Vermeule, pp. 169-71; Whitney 1976, pp. 260-61.

248. **American Numismatic Society, 1910**
Member's Medal
Struck silver (Tiffany & Co.), 76 mm

Gift of Mrs. Joseph F. Simmons and gift of David R. Lit from the collection of Victor D. Brenner
AJN 44 (1910), p. 130; ANS History, p. 184; Belden, pp. 60-61

249. The New Theatre, New York, 1910
Struck, gilt bronze, 89 mm

American Academy and Institute of Arts and Letters
IECM 1

250. American Red Cross Medal and Badge, 1911
Struck (different reverses): bronze, 70 mm; bronze, 40 mm

Eidlitz bequest

251. **David Livingstone Centenary Medal, 1915**
American Geographical Society
Struck (Tiffany & Co.): bronze, 75 mm; gilt bronze, 75 mm

On deposit from the American Geographical Society
AJN 49 (1915), pp. 200, 202

252. Independence Day, 1915
For Merit from the City of New York
Struck bronze (Medallic Art Co.), 38 mm

Gift of Medallic Art Co.
AJN 49 (1915), p. 202

251

Europe Comes to America

The International Exhibition of Contemporary Medals, New York, 1910

The International Exhibition of Medallic Art held by the American Numismatic Society in March 1910 presented the American public with an unprecedented opportunity to view about 2,400 medals by over 190 of the leading European and American medalists of the day. During its three week run, the Exhibition attracted a remarkable number of visitors, and it received favorable notice in the local press. A. Piatt Andrew, the Director of the U.S. Mint, wrote that "As an exhibition of modern medals it was unique in its variety and completeness, and as an indication of the awakening of American appreciation in a field of art hitherto neglected it was equally significant."

Among the artists singled out by Andrew for comment were the French medalists Chaplain and Roty, the Austrians Marschall and Kautsch, the Belgian Devreese and the English engraver Spicer-Simson. In general, the reviews of the Exhibition focused more on the achievements of the European medalists than on the work of their American counterparts. It is significant in this respect that the Committee of Award for the Exhibition, which included American sculptors Herbert Adams, Daniel Chester French and Hermon MacNeil, selected Belgian medalist Godefroid Devreese as Commemorative Medalist for 1910, "for having presented the most successful exhibit." As the recipient of this honor, Devreese was commissioned to produce a commemorative medal for the Exhibition, accompanied by a stipend of three thousand dollars. The resulting design was so disappointing that only three examples of the piece were ever struck (*253*). Using the rectangular plaquette format, Devreese created for the two sides of the medal a pair of banal allegorical compositions in the French manner, which have little to do with the subject matter of the Exhibition. The obverse of the medal depicts a female personification of America, who holds up a laurel branch and the U.S. flag and stands on a globe, facing a nude male figure reclining on a bank of clouds, carrying a lyre, symbolic of the arts. On the reverse, a female figure representing Liberty appears, rushing in on the back of an eagle which flies through a bank of clouds.

BIBLIOGRAPHY: ANS History, pp. 165-67, 184-85; A. Piatt Andrew, "An International Medallic Exhibition," *The American Review of Reviews* 41 (1910), pp. 561-67, excerpted in *The Numismatist* 23 (1910), pp. 173-74; IECM.

253. **International Medallic Exhibition Commemorative Plaquette, 1911**
American Numismatic Society
Godefroid Devreese
Struck bronze, 88 x 49 mm

ANS History, pp. 166, 184-85; Belden, pp. 62-63; IECM, pp. 5-6; de Witte 98

Godefroid Devreese (1861-1941)

Born at Courtrai, Belgium, Godefroid Devreese was trained as a sculptor from an early age in the studio of his father, the sculptor Constant Devreese. In 1881 he went to Brussels to study at the Académie Royale des Beaux-Arts with the sculptors Eugène Simonis and Charles van der Stappen, a friend of Roty. Devreese was awarded many honors and important commissions for medals and coins in his native country, and his work was also popular in this country, as witnessed by the articles on him which appeared in the *American Journal of Numismatics* in 1908 and 1910 and by his selection as Commemorative Medalist of the 1910 International Medallic Exhibition.

Devreese's medals and plaquettes are eclectic in style, drawing on both native traditions of the Low Countries and contemporary French medallic art as sources. His 1902 medal for the Association Belge de Photographie (**254**) and the 1906 plaquette L'aïeule (*257*), as well as a number of his other works, depict scenes of everyday life, inspired by the Flemish tradition of genre painting. The touching image of an old woman peeling a potato in front of a hearth on the 1906 piece recalls similar compositions in seventeenth-century paintings, both in the humble treatment of the theme and in its soft, painterly style, which shows the influence of Roty. Other medals by Devreese, for example his 1905 plaquette commemorating the architect Henri

257

Beyaert (**256**) and his commemorative plaquette for the 1910 International Medallic Exhibition (***253***), are executed in a more decorative, academic style. Both of these pieces feature classicizing allegorical compositions, comparable to the standard French work of the period, with much attention given to the modeling of the elaborate draperies that cling to the bodies of the figures.

BIBLIOGRAPHY: Agnes Baldwin, "M. Godefroid Devreese," *AJN* 44 (1910), pp. 61-63, pls. 6-11; Forrer, vol. 1, pp. 574-77, vol. 7, p. 221; IECM, pp. 72-79; Jones, pp. 138-39; J. de Lagerberg, "Medals by Godefroid Devreese," *AJN* 43 (1908/9), pp. 50-51; *The Studio* 33 (1904), pp. 264-65; Alphonse de Witte, "Godefroid Devreese, médailleur; biographie et catalogue de son oeuvre," *Gazette numismatique française* 7 (1903), pp. 337-53 and 15 (1911/2), pp. 121-80.

254. Association Belge de Photographie, 1902
Struck silver (Paul Tisch), 66 x 35 mm
Baldwin 5; IECM 4; de Witte 16

255. Alphonse de Witte, 1902
Société Hollandaise-Belge des Amis de la Médaille d'Art
Struck bronze (uniface), 67 x 46 mm
Eidlitz bequest
Baldwin 17; Dompierre de Chaufepié, p. 95; IECM 2; de Witte 45

256. Henri Beyaert, Architect, 1905
Galvano (Janvier & Duval, Paris), silvered copper, 136 x 84 mm
Eidlitz bequest
Baldwin 6; Dompierre de Chaufepié, p. 145; Eidlitz 83; IECM 22; de Witte 116

***257.* L'aïeule (The Grandmother), 1906**
Galvano, silvered copper, 85 x 98 mm
Baldwin 44; IECM 27; de Witte 113

258. Salomé, 1910
Société Hollandaise-Belge des Amis de la Médaille d'Art
Struck bronze, 93 x 45 mm
Baldwin 41; IECM 44; de Witte 84

259. Ernest Babelon/1910 International Numismatic Congress, Brussels, 1911
American Numismatic Society and Société Hollandaise-Belge des Amis de la Médaille d'Art
Obverse by Devreese, reverse by Rudolf Bosselt
Struck silver, 64 mm
Gift of Medallic Art Co.
ANS History, p. 185; Belden, pp. 64-65; de Witte 96

260. Silver Refinery at Hoboken-lez-Anvers, 1912
Struck bronze, 51 x 72 mm

261. Adolphe Greiner, Director of John Cockerill Co., 1912
Struck bronze, 80 x 52 mm

262. Premiere of *Parsifal* in Brussels, 1914
Struck bronze, 75 mm

Heinrich Kautsch (1859-1943)

The son of a Prague goldsmith, Heinrich Kautsch studied at the Imperial Schools of Decorative Arts in Prague and Vienna. After travels in Italy, France, and Germany, he returned in 1882 to Prague, where he became a professor at the Imperial School of Decorative Arts. In 1889 he settled in Paris, and he worked there for the rest of his life. A highly regarded medalist and sculptor, Kautsch served as a member of the Jury of Fine Arts at the 1893 Chicago World's Fair and as Vice-President of the Jury at the 1900 Paris Exposition. His work was awarded gold medals at the Universal Expositions in St. Louis in 1904 and Liège in 1905.

Kautsch's medals reveal an imaginative decorative sensibility, shaped by contact with the Austrian *art nouveau* movement, known as the Vienna Secession. In works such as his medals of the German poet Heinrich Heine (**263**) and the Munich painter Franz von Lenbach (***266***), Kautsch revitalizes the French allegorical idiom through his expressive modeling and use of artistic lettering in the Vienna Secession style. His vigorous portrait of

266

Lenbach is rich in texture and pictorial detail. The reverse of the Lenbach medal reworks an allegorical composition with antecedents in the oeuvre of Roty, which shows a female figure representing Painting seated in an attitude of reverie before a distant view of the artist's home town. Beside the unmistakably Viennese forms of the lettering in the inscription, Kautsch's clever treatment of the composition, constructed from an intriguing series of overlapping planes, and his sensuous modeling distinguish his work from that of Roty.

BIBLIOGRAPHY: Forrer, vol. 3, pp. 126-30, vol. 7, pp. 496-97; IECM, pp. 157-61; August Ritter von Loehr, *Wiener Medailleure*, vol. 2 (Vienna, 1902), pp. 59-61; Marx 1901, p. vi, pl. 26; *The Studio* 32 (1904), pp. 254, 256-58, and 35 (1905), pp. 238, 241-42.

263. Heinrich Heine, 1900
Galvano of reverse, silvered copper, 104 x 62 mm; struck, silvered bronze, 75 x 45 mm

Dompierre de Chaufepié, p. 115; IECM 16; Jones, p. 131; *The Studio* 32 (1904), pp. 254, 256

264. Paris Receiving Bosnia and Herzegovina, 1900
Bosnian Pavilion at the 1900 Paris Exposition
Struck silver, 80 x 99 mm

Bequest of Dr. George F. Kunz
IECM 24; Loehr 16

265. Chambre Syndicale de l'Automobile, 1903
Struck bronze (uniface), 56 x 75 mm

Dompierre de Chaufepié, p. 134; IECM 8

***266.* Franz von Lenbach, 1903**
Struck: silvered bronze, 85 x 60 mm; bronze, 64 x 45 mm

Eidlitz bequest and gift of Daniel M. Friedenberg
Dompierre de Chaufepié, p. 133; IECM 14; *The Studio* 32 (1904), pp. 254, 257

267. Margo Lenbach, 1905
Struck bronze (uniface), 60 mm

Gift of Daniel M. Friedenberg
Dompierre de Chaufepié, p. 133; IECM 21; *The Studio* 32 (1904), pp. 254, 258

268. A. Bartholomé, 1905
Struck, silvered bronze, 77 x 99 mm

Eidlitz bequest
Dompierre de Chaufepié, p. 133; IECM 1; *The Studio* 35 (1905), p. 241

Anton Scharff (1845-1903)

Anton Scharff was born in Vienna, where his father was a medalist at the Imperial and Royal Mint and an engraver of fine stones. In 1860, Scharff entered the Imperial School of Decorative Arts to study engraving, and in 1862 he was accepted to the Graveurakademie des Hauptmunzamtes, the "Academy of Engraving" attached to the Vienna Mint. He also studied modeling at the Akademie der bildenden Künste in Vienna. In 1866 he became an assistant engraver at the Imperial and Royal Mint, two years later he was promoted to the position of engraver, and in 1881 he was named director of the Graveurakademie. The culmination of Scharff's successful career at the Vienna Mint came in 1887, when the title *k. und k. Kammermedailleur*, "Court Medalist," was bestowed on him. A very prolific medalist, Scharff was the recipient of many awards and honors, including the Grand Prize at the Paris Exposition in 1900.

The sensitively modeled portrait of a Vienna laundry maid which Scharff first issued in 1878 as a medallion (**269**) established him as an artist in his own right. This popular genre piece was later reissued as a small, struck medal by the Austrian Society for the Promotion of Medallic Art. As Mark Jones has observed, Scharff's "fluent talent" brought him international recognition, and he was called upon to execute numerous medals for patrons in America and England, including Queen Victoria. The medals commissioned from him by American patrons (**270-71**, ***272***, and **273**) feature carefully observed portraits and tasteful allegorical compositions, modeled in a lively manner that saves them from banality. For example, his medal commemorating the first American statue of Gutenberg (***272***), erected in New York by Robert Hoe in 1899, is impressive for its rippling surfaces and exquisite handling of the textures of the printer's costume and beard. As this piece testifies, the turn-of-the-century developments in Viennese art that influenced Kautsch's style had no impact on Scharff's work, although he was in closer proximity to them.

BIBLIOGRAPHY: Carl Domanig, "Anton Scharff, k. und k. Kammer-Medailleur," *Numismatische Zeitschrift* 1894, pp. 271-320; Forrer, vol. 5, pp. 358-74, vol. 7, p. 191, vol. 8, p. 360; Jones, pp. 136-37; August Ritter von Loehr, *Wiener Medailleure*, vols. 1 and 2 (Vienna, 1899 and 1902), pp. 17-30, 51-53, and *Anton Scharff: Katalog seiner Medaillen und Plaketten* (Vienna, 1904); Marx 1901, p. vii, pl. 21.

269. Viennese Laundry Maid, 1878
Galvano, copper, 126 mm; reissue by the Oesterreichische Gesellschaft zur Förderung der Medaillenkunst und Kleinplastik, 1903: struck silver (uniface), 48 mm

Silver, gift of David R. Lit from the collection of Victor D. Brenner
Dompierre de Chaufepié, p. 33; IECM, p. 223, no. 6; Loehr 37

270. Samuel P. Avery, 1897
Cast bronze (uniface), 115 mm; struck silver, 65 mm

Silver, Eidlitz bequest
Loehr 282; *The Numismatist* 18 (1905), pp. 7-8

271. Ioannes S. White, 1897
Struck: silver, 65 mm; bronze, 65 mm

Dompierre de Chaufepié, pp. 36, 112; Loehr 295

***272.* Johann Gutenberg, 1899**
Gutenberg statue in New York by Robert Hoe
Struck: silver, 70 mm; bronze, 70 mm

Silver, gift of Daniel M. Friedenberg
Dompierre de Chaufepié, p. 98; Loehr 344

273. George Washington/Hall of Fame for Great Americans, New York, 1900
Struck: silver, 70 mm; bronze, 70 mm

Silver, gift of George R. Marvin
Dompierre de Chaufepié, p. 98; Loehr 350

272

Theodore Spicer-Simson (1871-1959)

Born at Le Havre, France, to English parents, Theodore Spicer-Simson began his art studies in London and then went to Paris, where he lived for many years. In Paris, he enrolled first at the Ecole des Arts Décoratifs and later studied at the Ecole des Beaux-Arts with the sculptor Jean-Auguste Dampt. From 1896 on, Spicer-Simson regularly exhibited his softly modeled portrait busts at the Paris Salons and the Royal Academy in London. He also pursued a strong interest in the decorative arts, designing book illustrations in the manner of Aubrey Beardsley (whose works he avidly collected) and working for Gorham & Co. in the United States at some time before 1903.

In 1903 Spicer-Simson began making cast portrait medallions, strongly reminiscent of the medals of the early Renaissance masters. One of the finest of his early medals, the medallion of artist George Frederick Watts executed in 1904 (***274***), was highly acclaimed for its bold Quattrocento conception and dignified, realistic likeness of the British painter. With its simple, cast surfaces and unelaborated composition, this piece more closely imitates the works of Pisanello and his followers than do the portrait medals by American sculptors (***77*** and ***233***, for example) based on the same models. In later portrait medals produced by the galvano technique, such as his 1911 medallion of Adra Newell (***278***), Spicer-Simson transforms his Renaissance sources by employing a more refined, decorative style, in the spirit of the English Aesthetic Movement. The portrait of Mrs. Newell is delicately modeled in extremely low relief, creating an elegant, almost precious, effect. In the years before the First World War, Spicer-Simson visited this country regularly, and after 1915 he settled permanently in New York, although he maintained his Paris studio.

BIBLIOGRAPHY: A. Darrall, "Theodore Spicer Simson," *Putnam's Monthly* 1 (1906/7), pp. 730-33; Forrer, vol. 5, pp. 600-610, vol. 8, pp. 213, 362; Henri Frantz, "Th. Spicer-Simson," *Art et Décoration* 14 (1903), pp. 297-301; E. Gimpel & Wildenstein Gallery, *Catalogue of an Exhibition of the Work of Spicer-Simson*, with a foreword by Edward T. Newell (New York, 1918); IECM, pp. 319-22; Jones, pp. 118-19; W. H. de B. Nelson, "Theodore Spicer-Simson, Medallist," *The International Studio* 64 (1918), pp. xxxvii-xliv; NSS 1923, pp. 232, 262; Theodore Spicer-Simson, "Portrait Reliefs, Medals and Coins in Their Relation to Life and Art," *AJN* 51 (1917), pp. 175-83.

274

***274.* George Frederick Watts, 1904**
Cast bronze (uniface), 115 mm
Gimpel & Wildenstein 1918, no. 61; IECM 18

275. Edward T. Newell, 1904
Cast bronze (uniface), 100 mm
IECM 11

278

276. Vice Admiral Sir Wilmot Hawksworth Fawkes, 1905
Cast bronze, 120 mm
Gimpel & Wildenstein 1918, no. 18; IECM 1

277. T. Spicer-Simson (Self-Portrait), 1907
Cast bronze (uniface), 67 mm
IECM 44

***278.* Adra Newell, 1911**
Galvano, gilt copper, 110 mm

279. A. Caro-Delvaille, 1916
Galvano, copper, 116 mm
Gimpel & Wildenstein 1918, no. 12

280. Alexander Agassiz Medal for Oceanography, undated
National Academy of Sciences
Struck bronze, 77 mm
Gimpel & Wildenstein 1918, no. 64

281. For Eminence in the Application of Science to the Public Welfare, undated
National Academy of Sciences
Struck bronze, 45 mm
Eidlitz bequest
Gimpel & Wildenstein 1918, no. 65

282. King Albert and Queen Elisabeth of the Belgians, 1918
American Numismatic Society
Struck (Medallic Art Co.): bronze, 63 mm; silver, 63 mm
ANS History, pp. 218-19; *The Numismatist* 31 (1918), pp. 430-31

283. Mary Clark Thompson Medal, 1920
National Academy of Sciences
Struck bronze, 76 mm
Gift of Wayte Raymond
The Numismatist 34 (1921), p. 201

284. Grace G. Scully, 1921
Cast bronze (uniface), 40 mm

Emil Fuchs (1866-1929)

Emil Fuchs was born in Vienna, where he studied sculpture at the Imperial Academy of Fine Arts. He later attended the Royal Academy in Berlin and received a traveling scholarship for study in Italy. Fuchs worked in Rome from 1891 until 1897, when he went to London at the behest of English patrons. His marble busts and small portrait medals,

285

which could be worn as jewelry or inserted in portable objects to be given as presents, became fashionable with the English aristocracy. Taking a fancy to an ashtray with one of Fuchs' medals in it which he had received as a gift, the Prince of Wales developed an interest in the artist's work and initiated a series of commissions by the Royal Family. Under the tutelage of John Singer Sargent, Fuchs also took up oil painting and became a prolific portrait painter. After 1905, he began to spend extended periods in New York, where he was in demand as a portraitist, and he later became a permanent resident of the United States.

His bust of Queen Victoria for the medal which she commissioned to celebrate the extension of her reign into the twentieth century (***285***) exemplifies Fuchs' soft, flattering style of portraiture. The delicate allegorical design on the reverse of this medal is also typical of his work. In his autobiography, the artist describes this reverse, which shows an angel carrying the name of the Queen around the world, as "a painting in light and shade." Fuchs achieves the desired painterly effect by modeling the composition in the lowest possible relief, blurring the edges of forms so that only the light glancing across the surface of the medal defines the image.

It is clear from his medals, as well as from his autobiography, that Fuchs admired the international elite whom he made a career of portraying. His plaquette memorializing J. P. Morgan (**292**) is an elegant panegyric to one of the wealthy men whom he described as "mile-stones in America's existence." A similar plaquette honoring metallurgist Robert Woolston Hunt (***294***) is of interest for the depiction of a steel mill on its reverse. While this image of workers and machinery should present a sharp contrast to the classicizing composition of the obverse, which features a pair of allegorical figures flanking a clipeate bust of Hunt, the artist's soft-edged style blurs the distinction between reality and ideality. Nevertheless, in comparison with the formality of the obverse, the reverse does have a more lively, sketchy quality, created by the subtle texturing of the surface and the use of incised lines to pick out certain details of the scene.

BIBLIOGRAPHY: Forrer, vol. 2, pp. 166-67, vol. 8, p. 349; Emil Fuchs, *With Pencil, Brush and Chisel: The Life of an Artist* (New York and London, 1925); Gardner, pp. 93-94; IECM, pp. 105-10; Mark Jones, "Emil Fuchs in England," *The Medal* 6 (1985), pp. 23-30; NSS 1923, pp. 81, 292-93, 356-57.

285. **Queen Victoria, 1900**
Commemorating her Reign in the New Century
Struck silver, 76 mm and 45 mm

Fuchs, pp. 106-107; IECM 28; *The International Studio* 20 (1903), p. 287

286. Queen Victoria, 1900
Struck silver, 35 mm

Fuchs, p. 106; IECM 29

287. The Princess of Pity, 1900
Struck silver, 40 x 40 mm

Fuchs, pp. 116-117

288. Coronation of Edward VII and Alexandra, 1902
Struck: silver, 64 mm; bronze, 64 mm

Bronze, Eidlitz bequest
IECM 4

289. Hispanic Society of America, 1906
Membership Medal
Struck: silver, 76 mm; bronze, 76 mm

Eidlitz bequest
IECM 12

290. Hispanic Society of America, 1907
Award Medal
Struck: silver (Tiffany & Co.), 101 mm; silver (Medallic Art Co.), 102 mm

Private collection, Brooklyn, New York, and gift of the Hispanic Society of America
IECM 11

291. Archer Milton Huntington Medal, 1908
50th Anniversary of the American Numismatic Society
Struck: bronze, 67 mm; silver, 67 mm

AJN 43 (1908/9), pp. 76-77; ANS History, pp. 176-77; Belden, pp. 46-47; IECM 2

292. John Pierpont Morgan, 1913
American Numismatic Society
Preliminary version, struck bronze, 74 x 90 mm; final version, struck bronze (Whitehead & Hoag Co.), 74 x 90 mm

ANS History, p. 186; Belden, pp. 66-67

293. Intercollegiate Current Events Contest, undated
The New York Times
Struck (Medallic Art Co.): bronze, 61 x 89 mm; silver, 61 x 89 mm

Eidlitz bequest
Stahl, pp. 2069-70

294. **Robert Woolston Hunt Medal, undated**
American Institute of Mining and Metallurgical Engineers
Struck (Medallic Art Co.): silvered bronze, 70 x 101 mm; bronze, 70 x 101 mm

294

The Metropolitan Museum of Art, 22.131 (gift of the American Institute of Mining and Metallurgical Engineers, 1922) and Eidlitz bequest
Gardner, p. 94; NSS 1923, pp. 292-93, 356

Jules Edouard Roiné (1857-1916)

A native of Nantes, France, J. Edouard Roiné studied with the local artist Chantron before going to Paris in 1877 to work with the sculptor Morice. In 1886 he moved to New York, where he worked primarily as a sculptor of architectural ornament and taught modeling at the Trade Mechanical School. He returned often to France, exhibiting his sculptures and medals yearly at the Paris Salons from 1895 to 1904 and receiving a gold medal for his work at the 1900 Paris Exposition.

The allegorical figure-compositions of Roiné's medals are very much in the French academic mold. As Alan Stahl has noted, the juxtaposition of classical and contemporary elements in Roiné's design for the medal of the Joseph K. Davison company (***296***), which features partially draped, nude figures operating the die cutting and reducing machines used by the firm, follows a precedent established by Roty. Roiné's debt to Roty is also evident in the rectangular format and soft-edged modeling of his Grover Cleveland commemorative medal (***302***), commissioned by the ANS. The overabundance of decorative detail and the awkward anatomy of the figures on the Cleveland medal detract from the effectiveness of the design and indicate some of the weaknesses of this style of medallic art.

BIBLIOGRAPHY: Forrer, vol. 5, pp. 195-96; IECM, pp. 263-66; Stahl, p. 2069.

295. Jour de Naissance, 1899
Struck silver, 41 mm
Eidlitz bequest
IECM 16

***296.* Joseph K. Davison's Sons, undated**
Struck bronze, 51 mm
Stahl, p. 2069

297. Gustav Killian, 1907
American Laryncological, Rhinological and Otological Society
Struck bronze, 63 mm
Eidlitz bequest

298. Algernon Sydney Sullivan, 1908
American Numismatic Society and New York State Bar Association
Struck bronze, 89 x 61 mm
Eidlitz bequest
IECM 2

299. Centenary of the Catholic Diocese of New York, 1909
Struck (Medallic Art Co.): silver, 76 mm; bronze, 76 mm
AJN 44 (1910), pp. 25-26; ANS History, p. 182; Belden, pp. 52-53; IECM 7

300. Abraham Lincoln Centennial, 1909
American Numismatic Society
Struck bronze (Whitehead & Hoag Co.), 102 x 73 mm
ANS History, p. 183; Belden, pp. 58-59; King 302

301. Abraham Lincoln, 1909
Struck from cancelled dies (Medallic Art Co.), white metal, 63 mm
AJN 43 (1908/9), pp. 23-24; King 310

***302.* Grover Cleveland, 1909**
American Numismatic Society
Struck (Medallic Art Co.): gold, 89 x 78 mm; silver, 89 x 78 mm
AJN 44 (1910), pp. 60-63; ANS History, p. 181; Belden, pp. 54-55; IECM 14

303. Lafayette Memorial Medal, 1911
Circle of Friends of the Medallion
Struck bronze (J.K. Davison's Sons), 77 x 48 mm
Gift of Daniel M. Friedenberg and Eidlitz bequest
Chamberlain, p. 129, fig. 52

304. Society of Beaux-Arts Architects, 1913
Struck bronze (Medallic Art Co.), 56 mm
Eidlitz bequest
AJN 47 (1913), pp. 149, 152-53

Isidore Konti (1862-1938)

Born in Vienna to Hungarian parents, Isidore Konti studied, like Fuchs, at the Austrian Imperial Academy. In 1886 he was awarded a traveling scholarship which enabled him to study in Italy for two years. He came to the United States in 1892

305

and worked briefly in New York with Philip Martiny, who sent him to Chicago to assist with the sculptural decoration for the World's Columbian Exposition. After his return to New York in 1893, Konti worked for several years with his friend Karl Bitter, another expatriate Viennese sculptor, before establishing his own studio. His allegorical sculptures for the Dewey Naval Arch erected in New York in 1899, the Pan-American Exposition of 1901, and the Louisiana Purchase Exposition of 1904 were highly acclaimed and brought him many further commissions. From 1914 until his death he lived and worked in Yonkers, New York.

Primarily a sculptor of architectural decoration, Konti created only a few medals in his spare time. His finest medallic work, the beautiful medal commemorating the 250th anniversary of Jewish settlement in the United States (***305***), illustrates the sculptor's love of graceful, feminine form. Thin veils of drapery flow softly around the statuesque female figures who symbolize the Jewish tradition and the reception of the Jews by America. Konti's exquisite low relief modeling and simple, harmonious compositions, free of excessive detail, make this a masterpiece of medallic art.

BIBLIOGRAPHY: Craven, pp. 475-77; Forrer, vol. 7, pp. 512-13; Gardner, pp. 79-80; IECM, pp. 162-64; A. S. Levetus, "Isidore Konti: A Hungarian Sculptor in America," *The International Studio* 45 (1912), pp. 200-203; Mary Jean Smith Madigan, *The Sculpture of Isidore Konti 1862-1938*, Hudson River Museum exhibition catalogue (Yonkers, 1975); NSS 1923, p. 130; Taft, pp. 463-65.

***305.* 250th Anniversary of Jewish Settlement in the U.S., 1905**
Struck: bronze, 76 mm; silver, 76 mm
National Numismatic Collection (Museum of American History, Smithsonian Institution) and Eidlitz bequest
IECM 2; Madigan 22

306. Isidor Memorial Medal, 1907
National Academy of Design
Struck silver, 40 mm
Eidlitz bequest
IECM 1; Madigan 24

307. Home Medal, 1910
Circle of Friends of the Medallion
Struck bronze (Medallic Art Co.), 70 mm
Eidlitz bequest
Chamberlain, pp. 128-29; Madigan 37

John Mowbray-Clarke (1869-1953)

John Mowbray-Clarke was born in Jamaica, West Indies, of British parents. The family returned to England while he was still a small boy, and he later received his formal training in sculpture at the Lambeth School of Art in London. Mowbray-Clarke came to the United States in 1896 and worked for two years with the sculptor J. Massey Rhind, before establishing his own studio in New York.

Although Mowbray-Clarke's medals are generally unexceptional, he was the only artist twice selected to design medals for the series issued by the Circle of Friends of the Medallion between 1909 and 1915 (**311** and ***312***). The American equivalent of the French, Belgian and Austrian organizations dedicated to the promotion of medallic art, the Circle of Friends sponsored the production of a dozen medals, which were issued in distinctive book-shaped holders with a text discussing the artist and the subject of the piece. Mowbray-Clarke's 1914 medal for the Circle of Friends, commemorating one hundred years of peace between Britain and America (***312***)—an appropriate subject for an expatriate British sculptor—is typical of his work in its soft modeling and prosaic, allegorical compositions. His treatment of the image of two nude male figures locked in combat on the obverse of this piece is much less forceful than John Flanagan's handling of the same Renaissance inspired motif on the obverse of his 1921 Verdun medal (***330***). The reverse, with its tame rendering of the American eagle and British lion who flank a dreamy female figure personifying Peace, is even weaker. This continental style of medallic art seems to have appealed to the members of the Circle of Friends, however, for they commissioned medals in a similar vein from several of the other immigrant European artists who worked in this country (**303** and **307**, for example).

BIBLIOGRAPHY: "Circle of Friends of the Medallion, 1909-1915," pp. 127-31 in Chamberlain; Forrer, vol. 8, pp. 85-86; IECM, p. 66; Charles de Kay, "Medals Issued by the Circle of Friends of the Medallion," *The Numismatist* 26 (1913), pp. 134-35.

308. Fred Wiley, 1906
Struck bronze (uniface), 101 mm
Eidlitz 1070

309. William Francklyn Paris, 1907
Cast bronze (uniface), 77 mm
Eidlitz bequest
Eidlitz 739

310. Abraham Lincoln/Justice, 1910
Struck bronze, 69 x 44 mm
Eidlitz bequest
King 787

311. Saint Brendan, 1911
Circle of Friends of the Medallion
Struck bronze (Jos. K. Davison's Sons), 70 mm
Gift of Daniel M. Friedenberg
Chamberlain, p. 129

***312.* 100 Years of Peace between Britain and America, 1914**
Struck bronze (Jos. K. Davison's Sons), 70 mm
Gift of Daniel M. Friedenberg
AJN 48 (1914), p. 212; Chamberlain, p. 131

312

World War I and beyond Beaux-Arts

317

World War I Medals

In his 1979 study of the medallic art of the First World War, *The Dance of Death*, Mark Jones has stressed the contrast between the war medals of the Allied nations and those produced by German medalists. While the Allied medalists "remained true to the elegant refinement of the pre-war tradition that had been common to all European medalists," their German counterparts abandoned the shared heritage of the "classical, post-Renaissance tradition" for a more forceful, expressive style. In general, the World War I medals by American artists bear out Jones' thesis in their use of ideal, allegorical compositions to represent the conflict.

Motivated by a desire to contribute to the war effort, the foremost American sculptors of the day, including artists who had not previously given much attention to medallic art, produced designs for war medals. Daniel Chester French, considered "the dean of American sculptors" by his contemporaries, had created few medals earlier in his career, but in his late sixties he designed the two most outstanding pieces (***317*** and ***327***) in the extensive series of war medals sponsored by the ANS. With its soft modeling and refined allegory, the beautiful head of Victory that he sculpted for the obverse of the ANS medal commemorating the visit of the French and British war commissions to New York in 1917 (***317***) stands firmly in the continental tradition of medallic art. By contrast, the design created for the reverse of this medal by French's former assistant Evelyn B. Longman is modeled in a more streamlined, hard-edged style, although it still features an allegorical figure-composition. One wonders if Longman's use of the figures of Joan of Arc and a medieval knight to represent France and England is a conscious response to the medieval symbolism employed by Karl Goetz and other German medalists in place of the classical vocabulary long favored by European medalists.

Another American World War I medal notable for its treatment of the classicizing, allegorical idiom is the piece by Adolph A. Weinman commemorating the war service of the Mount Sinai Hospital field unit (***328***). Weinman's lucid style and mastery of medallic composition give renewed dramatic force to the Greco-Roman imagery of a wounded warrior who is protected by a woman with attributes of the goddess Athena from a menacing German soldier grasping a huge serpent. By comparison, John Flanagan's representation of the battle of Verdun as a struggle between two Michelangelesque nude giants (***330***) is more distanced and less effective at conveying a sense of the real conflict, although the figures are powerfully modeled. Flanagan's design was selected over many others (**331** and **332** for example) submitted in a 1921 competition for the official medal to be presented by the people of the United States to the city of Verdun. The depiction of the medieval battlements of Verdun on the reverse of the Flanagan medal was an assigned feature of the piece and hence appears in the competition designs by other artists as well.

The nation's leading sculptors were also called

318

upon to design some of the decorations awarded to the American soldiers who had taken part in the Great War (***318***, **323**, **324**, and **329**, for example). An attractive piece by New York sculptor Allen G. Newman (1875-1940) won the National Arts Club competition for a Valor Medal (***318***) awarded for bravery. The sensuous personification of America and the majestic bald eagle skillfully modeled by Newman for this piece are very much in the Beaux-Arts tradition. At the close of the war, a Victory Medal was designed to be presented to every soldier who had fought for the Allied cause. Working from a standard format, an artist in each of the Allied nations executed a version of the medal for his countrymen in the soft-edged international style, varying the prescribed figure of Victory as he saw fit. For the U.S. version of the medal (**329**), sculptor James Earle Fraser created an uninspired allegorical figure, overloaded with attributes, which bears the combined features of Victory and the American Liberty.

BIBLIOGRAPHY: Mark Jones, *The Dance of Death: Medallic Art of the First World War*, British Museum pamphlet series (London, 1979); Evans E. Kerrigan, *American War Medals and Decorations* (New York, 1964; rev. ed., 1971); Ferriss Powell Merritt, "Distinguished Service Honors, U.S. Navy," *The Numismatist* 33 (1920), pp. 394-95; Frank Owen Payne, "The Present War and Sculptural Art," *Art and Archaeology* 8 (1919), pp. 17-38.

313. The Allied Bazaar for Liberty and Civilization, 1916
John Flanagan
Cast bronze (uniface), 170 x 113 mm

314. Study for a War Relief Medal (?), 1916
Adolph A. Weinman
Cast (uniface), gilt bronze, 77 mm
Gift of Mrs. Howard K. Weinman

315. America's War Medal, 1917
Theodore Spicer-Simson
Struck bronze, 31 mm
E. Gimpel & Wildenstein Gallery, *Catalogue of an Exhibition of the Work of Spicer-Simson* (New York, 1918), no. 71; *The International Studio* 64 (1918), pp. xxxix, xlii; *The Numismatist* 30 (1917), p. 330

316. American Declaration of War, 1917
American Numismatic Society
Eli Harvey
Struck silver (Medallic Art Co.), uniface, 88 mm
ANS History, pp. 215-16

***317*. Visit to New York of the French and British War Commissions, 1917**
American Numismatic Society
Obverse by Daniel Chester French, reverse by Evelyn B. Longman
Struck bronze (Medallic Art Co.), 63 mm
ANS History, p. 217; Hill 1984, p. 48, no. 30; NSS 1923, pp. 290, 356; Payne, pp. 34-35

***318*. U.S. Valor Medal, 1917**
National Arts Club
Allen G. Newman
Cross-shaped, struck bronze (Tiffany & Co.), 38 x 38 mm
NSS 1923, pp. 308, 360; *The Numismatist* 30 (1917), p. 370; Payne, pp. 27, 35

319. International Celebration of Independence Day, 1918
American Numismatic Society
Allen G. Newman
Struck: bronze, 63 mm; silver, 63 mm
Bronze, gift of Daniel M. Friedenberg
ANS History, pp. 217-18; NSS 1923, p. 360; *The Numismatist* 32 (1919), pp. 327-28

320. Williams College War Service Medal, 1918
James Earle Fraser
Struck bronze (Medallic Art Co.), 72 mm
Eidlitz bequest
NSS 1923, pp. 286, 355; *The Numismatist* 32 (1919), p. 448

321. Peace of Versailles, 1919
American Numismatic Society
Chester Beach
Struck silver (Medallic Art Co.), 63 mm
Gift of Robert A. Weinman from the collection of Adolph A. Weinman

ANS History, p. 219; NSS 1923, pp. 271, 351; *The Numismatist* 32 (1919), pp. 256-57; Vermeule, pp. 166-67

322. War and Peace, 1919
Emil Fuchs
Struck (Cartier): silver, 69 x 48 mm; bronze, 69 x 48 mm

Eidlitz bequest
NSS 1923, p. 356

323. U.S. Navy Distinguished Service Cross, 1919
James Earle Fraser
Cross-shaped, struck bronze, 38 x 38 mm

Kerrigan, p. 16; Merritt, pp. 394-95; NSS 1923, pp. 286, 355

324. U.S. Navy Distinguished Service Medal, 1919
Paul Manship
Struck bronze, 38 mm

Kerrigan, p. 21; Frederick D. Leach, *Paul Howard Manship, an Intimate View* (St. Paul, Minn., 1972), no. 20S; Merritt, pp. 394-95; Edwin Murtha, *Paul Manship* (New York, 1957), no. 118

325. Marion, Massachusetts, War Service Medal, 1920
John Flanagan
Cross-shaped, struck bronze, 41 x 41 mm

NSS 1923, pp. 285, 354; *The Numismatist* 33 (1920), p. 526

326. Army and Navy Chaplain's Medal, 1920
Laura Gardin Fraser
Struck bronze (Gorham & Co.), 70 mm

National Numismatic Collection (Museum of American History, Smithsonian Institution)
Ferriss Powell Merritt, "The Chaplain's Medal," *The Numismatist* 33 (1920), pp. 240-41; NSS 1923, p. 356

327. American Red Cross War Council (1917-1919), 1920
American Red Cross and American Numismatic Society
Daniel Chester French
Struck bronze (Medallic Art Co.), 70 mm

ANS History, p. 223; NSS 1923, pp. 291, 356; *The Numismatist* 34 (1921), p. 69

328. Mount Sinai Hospital War Unit (1917-1919), 1920
Adolph A. Weinman
Struck bronze (Medallic Art Co.), 76 mm; struck cliché of obverse, bronze, 76 mm

Cliché, gift of Mrs. Howard K. Weinman
NSS 1923, pp. 318, 362; Sydney P. Noe, *The Medallic Work of A. A. Weinman*, ANSNNM 7 (New York, 1921), pp. 42-43; *The Numismatist* 34 (1921), p. 300; Vermeule, p. 144

330

329. U.S. World War I Victory Medal, 1920
James Earle Fraser
Struck bronze, 36 mm

Kerrigan, pp. 88-90; *The Numismatist* 33 (1920), pp. 352-53

***330.* Verdun Medal, 1921**
From the People of the U.S. to the City of Verdun
John Flanagan
Uniface casts of obverse and reverse, bronze, 102 mm

Jones, *Dance of Death*, p. 11; NSS 1923, pp. 284, 355; *The Numismatist* 35 (1922), p. 132; Vermeule, pp. 124-25

331. Competition Design for the Verdun Medal, 1921
Anthony de Francisci
Uniface casts of obverse and reverse, gilt bronze, 99 mm

National Museum of American Art, Smithsonian Institution, 1966.51.62 and 1966.51.73 (gifts of Mrs. Anthony de Francisci)
NSS 1923, p. 353

332. Competition Design for the Verdun Medal, 1921
Paul Manship
Cast bronze, 102 mm

Gift of Paul Manship and Albert Gallatin; National Museum of American Art, Smithsonian Institution (gift of Paul Manship)

333. Defense of Verdun Medal, 1921
Awarded for Excellent Service in the U.S. Marine Corps
Paul Manship
Cast bronze, 102 mm

National Museum of American Art, Smithsonian Institution (gift of Paul Manship)
Frederick D. Leach, *Paul Howard Manship, An Intimate View* (St. Paul, Minn., 1972), no. 28S; Minnesota Museum of Art, *Paul Manship: Changing Taste in America* (St. Paul, Minn., 1985), p. 151, no. 111; Edwin Murtha, *Paul Manship* (New York, 1957), no. 141

Karl Goetz (1875-1950)

Born in Augsburg, Germany, Karl Goetz first attended the school of art in his home city and later studied in Dresden, Leipzig, Berlin, and Düsseldorf. In 1897 he went to Utrecht, Holland, and in 1899 to Paris, where he worked for five years. On his return to Germany in 1904, he settled in Munich, establishing himself in the succeeding decade as his country's leading medalist.

Goetz's early medals (**334**, for example) are stylistically related to the refined work of the Austrian court medalists Scharff and Marschall. By the time of his 1909 Darwin medal (**335**), however,

339

a new satirical element and a more direct realism are apparent in his work. These characteristics intensified with the advent of the World War, as Goetz turned his energies to attacking the Allies and promoting the German cause. The caustic satire and brutal realism of pieces like his *Lusitania* (*339*) and Verdun (*340*) medals are far removed from the elegant classicism of Allied war medals, and Goetz in fact directly mocks the allegorical symbolism of the French tradition in a number of his medals (**341**, for example). In contrast to the "emotional neutrality'' of John Flanagan's Verdun medal (*330*), Goetz's Verdun medal, which shows Britain as a pipe-smoking skeleton obscenely kneeing a captive France, is filled with ''naked hatred'' (Jones). The macabre figure of Death that appears over and over again in the medallic compositions of Goetz and his German contemporaries illustrates their turn away from the classical artistic tradition which had prevailed since the Renaissance in Europe to medieval, Germanic sources. In his choice of subject matter, his graphic style, and his manipulation of the emotions of the viewer, Goetz must be seen as part of the larger German expressionist art movement, as Cora Lee Gillilland has argued.

While Goetz's style of medallic art had little impact on American war medals, with the exception of a unique satirical piece by Paul Manship (*365*), the subject matter of his medals did provoke a great deal of reaction in this country, as well as in Britain and France. A quarter of a million copies of Goetz's *Lusitania* medal (*339*), depicting the ship's passengers at the Cunard Lines office buying their tickets from Death and the sinking ocean liner spilling over with weapons, were produced in England and distributed also in the U.S. as evidence of the callousness of the German ''War Lords.'' The text accompanying the English copy of the medal even seizes on the incorrect dating of the incident to May 5, rather than May 7, on Goetz's original version of the piece as proof of the Germans' ''premeditated and premature jubilation at the fate of innocent civilians.''

BIBLIOGRAPHY: Howard L. Adelson and Louis L. Snyder, ''National Myths in the Weimar Republic: An Iconographic Study,'' *ANSMN* 8 (1958), pp. 189-216; Forrer, vol. 7, pp. 379-86; Cora Lee C. Gillilland, ''Karl Goetz: His Place within the History of Medallic Art,'' *The Numismatist* 89 (1976), pp. 485-97; George F. Hill, *The Commemorative Medal in the Service of Germany* (London, 1917); Jones, pp. 146-48; Jones, *The Dance of Death* (London, 1979); Gunter W. Kienast, *The Medals of Karl Goetz*, 2 vols. (Cleveland, Ohio, 1967 and 1986).

334. Ernst von Possart, 1905
Cast bronze (uniface), 89 x 68 mm
Gift of Ira, Lawrence, and Mark Goldberg
Kienast, opus 37

335. Charles Robert Darwin Centennial, 1909
Cast bronze, 70 mm; iron trial cast of reverse, 85 mm
Gift of Ira, Lawrence, and Mark Goldberg
Kienast, opus 57

336. The Mobilization of the German Army, 1914
Cast bronze, 84 mm
Gift of Ira, Lawrence, and Mark Goldberg and gift of Wayte Raymond
Kienast, opus 134

337. American Neutrality, 1914/5
Cast bronze, 56 mm
Benjamin Sillins collection gift and gift of Ira, Lawrence, and Mark Goldberg
Gillilland, pp. 487, 489; Hill, fig. 17; Kienast, opus 149; *The Numismatist* 29 (1916), pp. 118-19

340

338. The Campaign of Lies of the Entente, 1914
Oblong, cast bronze, 60 x 90 mm
Gift of Ira, Lawrence, and Mark Goldberg
Hill, fig. 8; Kienast, opus 141

339. The Sinking of the *Lusitania*, 1915
Cast bronze, 56 mm; replica, struck lead, 56 mm

Bronze, gift of Christian Ebsen and gift of George H. Clapp; lead, gift of Albert E. Gallatin and gift of Mrs. George N. Hamilton in memory of Col. George N. Hamilton
Adelson and Snyder, pp. 190-92; Hill, pp. 21-24, fig. 11; Jones, *Dance of Death*, pp. 17-19; Keinast, vol. 1, pp. 13-18, opus 156; *The Numismatist* 29 (1916), p. 215

340. **Verdun, 1917**
Cast bronze, 58 mm
Gift of Ira, Lawrence, and Mark Goldberg
Jones, *Dance of Death*, pp. 12, 13; Kienast, Opus 196

341. The Robber's Court in Mainz, 1923
Cast bronze, 60 mm
Benjamin Sillins collection gift and gift of Ira, Lawrence, and Mark Goldberg
Kienast, opus 296

Anthony de Francisci (1887-1964)

Anthony de Francisci was born in Italy and came as a young man to New York, where he studied with George Brewster at the Cooper Union, with James Earle Fraser at the Art Students League, and at the National Academy of Design. Upon completion of his studies, he was employed as a studio assistant by the sculptors Martiny, MacNeil, Niehaus, and, most importantly, Adolph A. Weinman, with whom he worked for six years. He later taught modeling at Columbia University's School of Architecture and at the Beaux-Arts Institute in New York.

347

De Francisci's medals and portrait reliefs carry the Saint-Gaudens tradition, handed down to him by Fraser and Weinman, beyond the First World War. In works such as his bas-relief portraits of Weinman (**343**) and Carmela Cafarelli (***347***), de Francisci shows a talent for modeling in the refined beaux-arts style. The Cafarelli portrait is particularly notable for its fluid surfaces, which softly reflect the light shining on them, emphasizing the feminine grace of the sitter. Other portraits of the artist's friends and relatives (**346**, for example) are modeled in a looser, sketchier style, reminiscent of some of Saint-Gaudens' portrait reliefs.

In his designs for medals, de Francisci closely follows Weinman's example. The reverses of his Douglas medal for the American Institute of Mining and Metallurgical Engineers (**345**) and his McGraw award medal for the Electrical Industry (***348***) are patterned after the innovative reverse of Weinman's Saltus award medal for the ANS (***182***), where a depressed circular field at the center of the composition is used to set off the pictorial motif from the surrounding inscriptions. De Francisci's spare, allegorical designs, populated by ideal, nude figures, also recall Weinman's medallic compositions. For the 1928 lifesaving medal of the Midland Utilities Company (**350**), the younger artist borrowed his mentor's discarded design for the 1906 U.S. Life Saving Medal (***172***), modernizing Weinman's composition by employing the bolder forms associated with the Art Deco style of the 1920s. This piece and the ANS medal produced by de Francisci in commemoration of the 150th anniversary of Paul Revere's historic ride (**349**) are original in their experimentation with the use of convex surfaces.

BIBLIOGRAPHY: Forrer, vol. 8, pp. 347-48; "The Medals of de Francisci," *National Sculpture Review* 8 (1959/60), pp. 14-15; NSS 1923, pp. 47, 278-79, 353.

342. Damiano Giuseppe Vuletich, 1913
Cast bronze (uniface), 95 x 83 mm

National Museum of American Art, Smithsonian Institution, 1966.51.93 (gift of Mrs. Anthony de Francisci)
NSS 1923, p. 353

343. Adolph Alexander Weinman, 1915
Cast (uniface), silvered bronze, 214 x 142 mm

National Museum of American Art, Smithsonian Institution, 1966.51.29 (gift of Mrs. Anthony de Francisci)
NSS 1923, p. 353

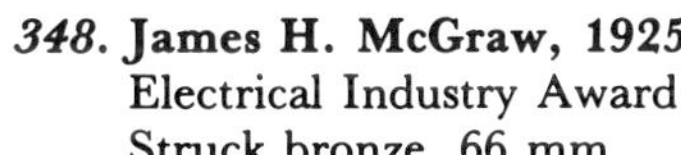

348. James H. McGraw, 1925
Electrical Industry Award
Struck bronze, 66 mm

349. Paul Revere Sesqui-Centennial, 1925
American Numismatic Society
Struck: bronze, 63 mm; silver, 63 mm

ANS History, pp. 224-25; *The Numismatist* 38 (1925), pp. 265-66

350. Midland Utilities Life Saving Medal, 1928
Struck bronze, 62 mm

348

344. British-American Cup Crew Medal, 1922
Struck clichés of obverse and reverse, gilt bronze, 76 mm

NSS 1923, pp. 278, 353; Vermeule, p. 152

345. James Douglas Award Medal, undated
American Institute of Mining and Metallurgical Engineers
Struck bronze, 69 mm
NSS 1923, pp. 279, 353

346. John Gregory, 1923
Cast bronze (uniface), 107 mm

National Museum of American Art, Smithsonian Institution, 1966.110.1 (gift of Mrs. Gilda Slate)

347. Carmela Chiostergi Cafarelli, 1923
Cast bronze (uniface), 201 mm

National Museum of American Art, Smithsonian Institution, 1966.110.8 (gift of Mrs. Gilda Slate)
(An example of this piece from the ANS collection is illustrated.)

Hermon Atkins MacNeil (1866-1947)

A native of Chelsea, Massachusetts, Hermon Atkins MacNeil studied sculpture at the Massachusetts Normal School of Art in Boston. Before going to Paris in 1888, he taught modeling and drawing for three years at Cornell University. In Paris, he continued his studies with Chapu at the Académie Julian and Falguière at the École des Beaux-Arts. On his return to the United States in 1891, he worked as an assistant to Philip Martiny on the architectural sculptures for the World's Columbian Exposition. After the Fair, MacNeil remained in Chicago for three years, teaching at the Art Institute and making several trips west to study Indians, who became the principal subject of his sculpture. In 1896 he won the Rhinehart Roman scholarship, which enabled him to spend three years working in Rome. When he returned to America, his Indian sculptures were enthusiastically received, and he became a very successful academic sculptor. MacNeil taught at the Pratt Institute in Brooklyn, the Art Students League, and for twelve years in the evening school of the National Academy of Design. He was twice elected to the presidency of the National Sculpture Society.

The few medals which MacNeil executed are of high quality. While his earlier medals are modeled in delicate, low relief in the Beaux-Arts tradition, his later medallic work makes the transition to the more hard-edged Art Deco style. The stylized snake dancers of MacNeil's 1931 Hopi medal (*354*) are

Eidlitz bequest
NSS 1923, pp. 300, 359

352. Poppenhausen Institute, 1918
Struck bronze (Medallic Art Co.), 64 mm
Eidlitz bequest
NSS 1923, p. 359

353. Tercentenary of the Purchase of Manhattan, 1926
American Numismatic Society and New York Historical Society
Struck silver, 63 mm
ANS History, pp. 225-26; "Tercentenary of New York Medals," pp. 138-40, fig. 2 in Chamberlain

354

in marked contrast to the more naturalistic Indian figures of his 1901 Pan-American Exposition medal (*106*). Although the figures are no longer individualized, the rhythm created by the sharp outlines and the repeated patterns in the design give the Hopi medal a sense of lively movement, making it a fine piece of decorative work.

BIBLIOGRAPHY: Adolph Block, "Hermon A. MacNeil," *National Sculpture Review* 12/3 (1963/4), pp. 17, 28; Craven, pp. 516-21; "The Designers of the New Silver Coinage," *AJN* 49 (1915), pp. 210-12; Forrer, vol. 8, pp. 15-16; Gardner, pp. 96-97; NSS 1923, pp. 158, 300-301, 359; Taft, pp. 437-45; Whitney 1976, p. 291.

351. Architectural League of New York, undated
Awards for Painting and Landscape Architecture
Struck bronze (Medallic Art Co.), 64 mm (with two variant reverses)

***354*. Hopi/Prayer for Rain, 1931**
Society of Medalists
Oblong, struck bronze (Medallic Art Co.), 69 x 73 mm

Laura Gardin Fraser (1889-1966)

Although she was born in Chicago, Laura Gardin went to high school in New York and studied briefly at Columbia University. She then enrolled at the Art Students League, where she studied from 1907 to 1910 with James Earle Fraser and worked for two more yearrs as an instructor. In 1913 she and Fraser were married, and they spent their later years living and working in Westport, Connecticut. Along with the more than one hundred medals to her credit, Laura Gardin Fraser holds the distinction of being the first woman to design a coin for any government, the Alabama Centennial half dollar of 1921. Three other issues of U.S. commemorative coinage—the 1922 Grant Centenary half dollar, and 1925 Fort Vancouver Centennial half dollar, and the 1926 Oregon Trail memorial half dollar, designed in collaboration with her husband—were

359

her work.

In the early 1920s, Fraser went from creating medals with "such appropriately feminine subjects" as Better Babies (**355**) to doing sensitively modeled animal subjects (**357** and **358**) (Vermeule). When her commemorative coins proved to be popular, she was called upon to design several important medals for the U.S. government. Laura Fraser's designs for the Congressional Medal presented to Charles A. Lindbergh (***359***) and the official George Washington Bicentennial medal (**360**) update the Renaissance models used by her husband in his medallic work. The streamlined style of the Lindbergh medal heralds the age of transatlantic aviation. Boldly simple in design, this piece is particularly notable for its "Lone Eagle" reverse, a modernized version of Saint-Gaudens' flying eagle composition for the 1907 U.S. twenty-dollar gold piece (***202***). Fraser's Washington Bicentennial medal is likewise based on a work by Saint-Gaudens, his 1889 Washington medal (***77***), but a comparison of the two pieces highlights the contrast between the soft, textured modeling of the earlier medal and the smooth surfaces and clearly delineated forms of the later piece.

BIBLIOGRAPHY: John W. Dunn, "Laura's Medals," *Coinage* 4, no. 11 (1977), pp. 32-34, 38, 40, 122, 124; Forrer, vol. 7, p. 321, vol. 8, pp. 348-49; Rena Tucker Kohlman, "America's Women Sculptors," *The International Studio* 76 (1922), p. 228; Dean Krakel, *End of the Trail* (Norman, OK, 1973); Ferriss Powell Merritt, "Laura Gardin Fraser, Artist, Sculptor," *The Numismatist* 33 (1920), p. 315; NSS 1923, pp. 69, 288-89, 356; William S. Nawrocki, "Laura Gardin Fraser's Numismatic Beauties," *Coinage* 17, no. 8 (1981), pp. 17-18, 120, 122, 124; Vermeule, pp. 163-65, 181-82.

355. Better Babies Award, 1913
Woman's Home Companion
Struck bronze (Medallic Art Co.), 50 mm
AJN 47 (1913), pp. 149, 152; NSS 1923, pp. 289, 356

356. Rosemary School Award Medal, 1915
Struck bronze (Medallic Art Co.), 63 mm
AJN 49 (1915), p. 204; NSS 1923, pp. 288, 356

357. Irish Setter Club of America, 1922
Struck bronze (Medallic Art Co.), 77 mm
Gift of the Irish Setter Club of America in memory of Warren Delano
NSS 1923, pp. 289, 356

358. Vermont, 1923
Struck (Medallic Art Co.), uniface, gilt bronze, 76 mm

***359.* Charles A. Lindbergh, 1929**
By act of U. S. Congress
Struck bronze (U.S. Mint), 69 mm
U.S. Mint 1972, no. 645

360. George Washington Bicentennial, 1932
Struck bronze (U.S. Mint), 76 mm and 56 mm
Large bronze, gift of the George Washington Bicentennial Commission
Harvey L. Hansen, "George Washington Bicentennial Celebration 1732-1932: A Metallic Record," *The Numismatist* 47 (1934), p. 4; Rulau and Fuld, pp. 221-22; U.S. Mint 1972, no. 610; Vermeule, pp. 181-82.

364

Paul Manship (1885-1966)

Paul Manship grew up in St. Paul, Minnesota, and studied there at the Institute of Art from 1892 until 1903. He moved to New York in 1905 and enrolled at the Art Students League, while working as an assistant in the studio of sculptor Solon Borglum, the brother of Gutzon Borglum. In 1907 he went to Philadelphia to study with Charles Grafly at the Pennsylvania Academy of Fine Arts, and the following year he worked as an assistant to Isidore Konti in New York. Manship was awarded the newly instituted Rome Prize for sculpture in 1909 and spent the next three years at the American Academy in Rome. A trip to Athens before his return to the United States in 1912 confirmed his appreciation of early Greek sculpture and influenced the direction of his work. From 1922 until 1926, Manship was again in Europe, working this time in Paris. In the 1940s, the popular sculptor taught at the Pennsylvania Academy of Fine Arts.

Manship's medals illustrate his development of a new style of sculptural art, related to the Art Deco movement of the 1920s and 1930s in its bold, decorative stylizations, but based on the study of an eclectic array of Italian Renaissance, archaic Greek, Egyptian and Indian sources. While Manship claimed that his designs for the 1916 medal of the St. Paul Art Institute (***364***), which feature Pegasus and a Muse holding a small Victory, represented a departure "from stereotyped models generally used in this connection," this piece and many of his other medals deviate little from the classical, allegorical vocabulary of the Beaux-Arts tradition. It is more in style and technique than iconography that his medals differ from Beaux-Arts works like James Earle Fraser's 1915 medal for the American Academy of Arts and Letters (**234**) which is similar in iconography to the St. Paul Institute medal. The kneeling Muse on the obverse of the St. Paul Institute medal, who resembles an Indian or Egyptian statue in pose, is sculpted in an appropriately archaizing, strongly linear style.

Manship's revival of the direct casting technique of Renaissance medals contributes to the bold impression of his designs. In this aspect of his medallic art he is comparable to Karl Goetz, who also preferred the rough finish obtained by casting, rather than striking, his medals. It is significant that Manship alone, with his graphic style, attempted an American answer to Goetz's satirical war medals in his 1918 piece Kultur in Belgium (***365***). The grotesque imagery of an obese Kaiser in war uniform wearing a "rosary" of human skulls around his neck and a brutish German soldier abducting a pleading Belgian woman was not well received in this country.

BIBLIOGRAPHY: Craven, pp. 565-68; Forrer, vol. 8, pp. 22-24; Albert E. Gallatin, *Paul Manship: A Critical Essay on his Sculpture and an Iconography* (New York, 1917), and "An American Sculptor: Paul Manship," *The Studio* 82 (1921), pp. 137-44; Gardner, pp. 150-54; Herbert L. Kammerer, "In Memoriam—Paul Manship," *National Sculpture Review* 14 (1965/66), p. 7; Frederick D. Leach, *Paul Howard Manship, an Intimate View*, catalogue of an exhibition at the Minnesota Museum of Art (St. Paul, MN, 1972); Minnesota Museum of Art, *Paul Manship: Changing Taste in America*, exhibition catalogue (St. Paul, Minn., 1985); Edwin Murtha, *Paul Manship* (New York, 1957); National Collection of Fine Arts and Saint Paul Art Center, *Paul Manship 1885-1966*, exhibition catalogue (Washington, D.C., 1966); NSS 1923, pp. 161, 305, 359; Smithsonian Institution, *A Retrospective Exhibition of Sculpture by Paul Manship* (Washington, D.C., 1958); Paul Vitry, *Paul Manship, sculpteur américain* (Paris, 1927); Whitney 1976, pp. 291-92.

361. New York Tercentenary, 1914
Circle of Friends of the Medallion
Struck bronze (Jos. K. Davison's Sons), 70 mm

Gift of Daniel M. Friedenberg
AJN 48 (1914), p. 212; Chamberlain, p. 131, fig. 54; Murtha 58; "Tercentenary of New York Medals," pp. 138-40 in Chamberlain

362. Civic Forum Medal for Distinguished Public Service, 1914
Cast bronze, 82 mm

Gift of Paul Manship
Murtha 57; NSS 1923, p. 359; *The Numismatist* 27 (1914), p. 249

***363*. Maxfield Parrish, 1915**
Cast bronze, 182 mm

Gift of Paul Manship
Leach 10S; Minnesota Museum of Art 1985, p. 150, no. 110; Murtha 65; NSS 1923, p. 359

***364*. St. Paul Institute, 1916**
Cast bronze, 128 mm; cast bronze, 54 mm

Small bronze, Eidlitz bequest
Leach 15S; Murtha 76; NSS 1923, pp. 305, 359

***365*. Kultur in Belgium, 1918**
Cast bronze (Medallic Art Co.), 66 mm

Gift of Albert Gallatin and gift of Daniel M. Friedenberg
Leach 18S; Minnesota Museum of Art 1985, p. 151, no. 112; Murtha 103; NSS 1923, p. 359; Frank Owen Payne, "The Present War and Sculptural Art," *Art and Archaeology* 8 (1919), pp. 25, 35

366. The French Heroes' Fund, 1918
Cast bronze (Medallic Art Co.), 65 mm

Gift of Albert Gallatin
Murtha 104

367. Welles Bosworth, Architect, 1920
Cast bronze, 93 mm

Gift of Paul Manship and Eidlitz bequest
Leach 24S; Murtha 125; NSS 1923, p. 359

***368*. Victory Medal, undated**
Art War Relief
Triangular, cast bronze mounted on wood, 99 x 81 mm

Gift of Albert Gallatin
NSS 1923, pp. 305, 359

365

The American Numismatic Society and the Beaux-Arts Medal

125

Medals played only a minor role in the activities of the American Numismatic Society in the first decades after its founding in 1858. They were acquired and discussed, but generally grouped with tokens, decorations and other objects whose coin-like form or manufacture placed them within the purview of numismatic institutions. Through 1890, the Society issued only five medals: one each in honor of Lincoln and Washington, a membership medal and two to honor its own presidents; three of these were from dies engraved in Sweden by Lea Ahlborn.

A change in attitude towards the medal appears to have arisen in connection with the Chicago World's Columbian Exposition of 1893, the impetus for so many developments in American art. After a survey of existing numismatic tributes to Columbus in response to an inquiry from the Società Geografica Italiana, the Society sponsored the striking of a Columbus medal by Tiffany & Co. "believing that no medal has thus far been made suitable to the occasion." In addition it organized an exhibition of medals of the Chicago Exposition which brought over 900 people in one day to the Society's premises.

In 1896, the Society's president "stated that it seemed to him a duty of the Society to commemorate important events of local interest by the striking of a medal." In the next three years the Society issued a medal by Tiffany to commemorate the dedication of Grant's Tomb, and medals for St. Luke's Hospital (**116**) and the National Conference of Charities and Corrections (***118***), both by its active member Victor D. Brenner. At a meeting in 1896, Walter Tonnele, a member of the Executive Committee, addressed the Society on "The Modern Renaissance of the Medallic Art," devoted mainly to the careers of Chaplain and Roty, and the following year Brenner gave a talk on "Art and the Medal," in which he singled out for special praise the work of Bottée.

Members of the Society had direct contact with the developments of the French medal at the Paris Exposition of 1900. Despite the objections of a former president who feared "that the medals produced in this country could not compete with those of France in artistic merit," the Society accepted the invitation to send an exhibit to Paris. It had the good fortune of having four of its members in France at that moment, including Augustus Saint-Gaudens and, especially, Victor Brenner, who took charge of setting up the 5 foot by 6 foot case of American coins, decorations and medals sent from New York. Member George Kunz reported on the Exposition to the members the following year, concentrating his account on a description of the extensive display of the French Mint, notable not only for the beautifully executed masterpieces by Roty and Chaplain, but for the low price at which tens of thousands of medals were sold to the public.

In 1900, the Society undertook the sponsorship of a school for die cutting and medal design, established in conjunction with the National Academy of Design. The school soon reached its projected enrollment of nine students under the instruction of Charles J. Pike, who is not known to have produced any medals. In the fall of 1901, Brenner, recently returned from Paris, replaced Pike and taught die engraving as well as modeling. Brenner directed the school for a year and then resigned; Pike was reappointed and taught classes for the next three years. It appears that the class failed to enroll serious professionals, although instruction in "ornamental decoration and artistic jewelry" was added in the hopes of attracting students who might then develop an interest in medals. None of the winners of student prizes is known to have gone on to design a produced medal, and in 1905 the school was discontinued.

Another ambitious project of this period was the plan to issue a series of medals of noted Americans, to be offered to members of the Society on an annual basis. The original plan for medals honoring one man in each of six fields of endeavor was soon changed to individuals who had offerered distinguished service in the discovery or development of America. The first medal in the series, of Amerigo Vespucci (***125***), appeared in 1903, after a delay caused by the search for an authentic portrait to serve as the basis for Brenner's depiction. A similar difficulty was encountered in the production of the Sir Francis Drake medal, the only other medal in the series.

In the meantime came many opportunities for medals tied to the commemoration of specific events. Of chiefly internal significance were two medals for the fiftieth anniversary of the Society, by Victor Brenner (**135**) and Emil Fuchs (**291**), and a new membership medal by Gutzon Borglum (***248***). Under its own initiative, the Society produced medals marking the visit to New York of Prince Henry of Prussia and the transfer of the body of John Paul Jones to Annapolis, both by Brenner.

302

Most of the thirty-five medals issued under the auspices of the American Numismatic Society between 1893 and 1926 were, in fact, the result of agreements with other institutions. The philosophy behind such arrangements was expressed in the 1909 report of the Committee on the Publication of Medals: "The seal of the Society upon a medal or plaque would then be sought by those who wished to provide commemorative medals; its facilities would be availed in the design and issue thereof; its vaults would become a depository of the dies; and the sculpture and other artistic societies, as well as historians in their various forms of organization, would actively support this Society in its several departments of artistic endeavor." President Huntington's plea at the same meeting that "the

248

subject of the medal must be secondary to its artistic value" was heeded in most cases; the artists commissioned include many of the major sculptors of the day. Their style ranges from the formal medals by Fuchs for the Hudson-Fulton Celebration (***99***) and Roiné for the death of Grover Cleveland (***302***), to the more inventive New Theatre medal of Pratt (***220***) and ANS Membership medal of Borglum (***248***).

The Society attracted the leading medalists of the day to membership and to its meetings. In 1919 a competition was held for the design of the J. Sanford Saltus medal, limited to those sculptors who were members of the Society; fifteen medalists submitted designs. The award medal, by A. A. Weinman (***182***), was designated for signal achievement in the art of the medal; it continues to be the most respected American award for medallic sculpture.

The high point of the involvement of the American Numismatic Society in medallic art was its 1910 International Exhibition of Contemporary Medals. From the time of its move in 1907 to its present home, the Society had been planning a major opening exhibition. It is indicative of the role which medals played in the period that this took the form of an exhibition of 2,400 works by contemporary medalists from Europe and America. A total of more than 5,500 people viewed the exhibition in the three weeks it was on view in the Society's hall and a temporary building next door. Many pieces on exhibit were purchased for the Society's collection and these, along with subsequent purchases and gifts, form the base for the present exhibition.

As the expositions in Chicago in 1893 and in Paris in 1900 can be seen as the impetus for the

Society's interest in medallic art and its own 1910 show as the high point, the final burst of enthusiasm can be seen in its shows of 1923 and 1924. In conjunction with the 1923 exhibition of the National Sculpture Society, the ANS mounted a display of work by contemporary American medalists. The next year it displayed works of Europeans produced since the 1910 show. By this time, however, the overall focus of the American Numismatic Society had shifted from a fellowship of collectors to that of a scholarly research institution whose main interest was the study of coins as historical evidence. Medals, especially contemporary ones, were to play an ever smaller role in the activities and publications of the institution, and from 1927 to 1971 only four medals were issued by the Society, three of which were for internal events. With the resurgence in recent years of interest in American art and in the contemporary medal, the American Numismatic Society has again turned its attention to medallic sculpture, as its sponsorship of the current exhibition demonstrates.

SOURCES: Manuscript and typescript minutes of the American Numismatic Society and its Executive Committee and Council; its published Proceedings and Papers; ANS History; Belden; IECM.

Alan M. Stahl
Curator of Medals
American Numismatic Society

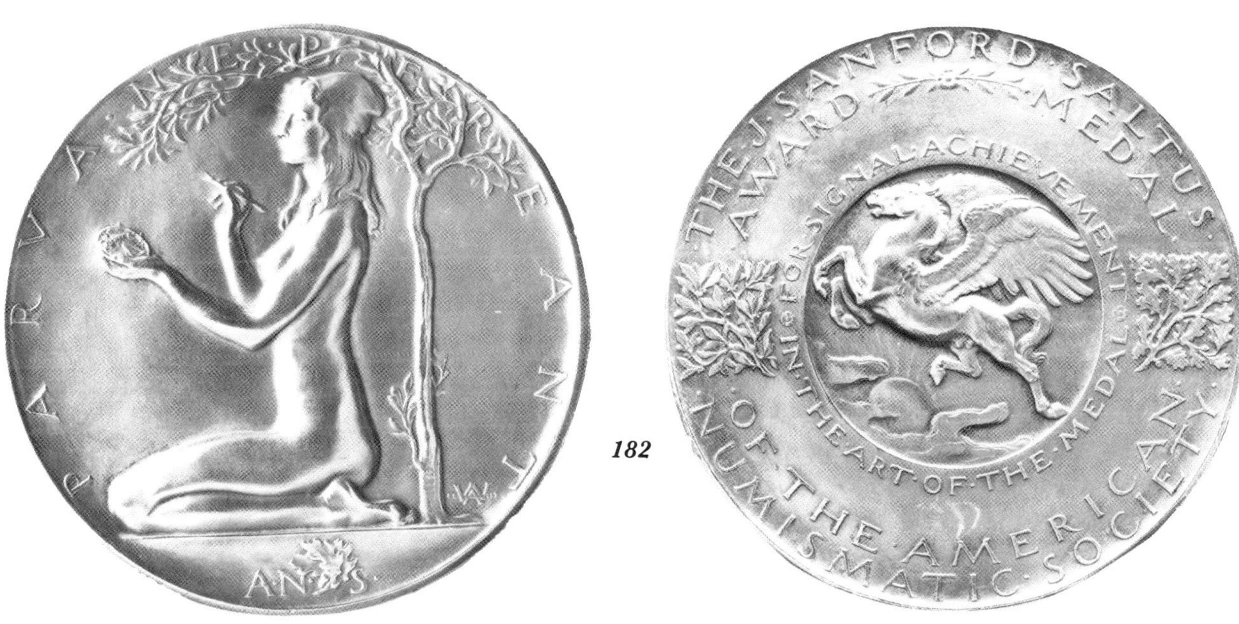

182

Bibliography and Abbreviations

AJN: *American Journal of Numismatics.*

ANSMN: *American Numismatic Society Museum Notes.*

ANSNNM: American Numismatic Society Numismatic Notes and Monographs.

ANS History: Adelson, Howard L. *The American Numismatic Society 1858-1958.* New York, 1958.

Belden: Belden, Bauman L. *Medals and Publications of the American Numismatic Society.* New York, 1915.

Benedite: Benedite, Leonce. *Le Musée National du Luxembourg: Catalogue Raisonné.* Paris, 1896.

Cat. gen.: *Catalogue général illustré des èditions de la Monnaie de Paris*, 4 vols. Paris, 1977—.

Chamberlain: Chamberlain, Georgia Stamm. *American Medals and Medalists.* Annandale, Virginia, 1963.

Craven: Craven, Wayne. *Sculpture in America.* New York, 1968.

Detroit 1983: Detroit Institute of Arts, *The Quest for Unity: American Art between the World's Fairs, 1876-1893.* Detroit, 1983.

Dompierre de Chaufepié: Dompierre de Chaufepié, H. J. de. *Les médailles et plaquettes moderns. 3 vols.* Harlem, 1901.

Eidlitz: Eidlitz, Robert James. *Medals and Medallions Relating to Architects.* New York, 1927.

Forrer: Forrer, Leonard. *Biographical Dictionary of Medalists.* 8 vols. London, 1902-1930.

Gardner: Gardner, Albert Ten Eyck. *American Sculpture: A Catalogue of the Collection of the Metropolitan Museum of Art.* New York, 1965.

Hibler and Kappen: Hibler, Harold E., and Kappen, Charles V. *So-Called Dollars.* New York, 1963.

Hill 1984: Hill, May Brawley. *The Woman Sculptor: Malvina Hoffman and her Contemporaries.* New York, 1984.

IECM: The American Numismatic Society, *Catalogue of the International Exhibition of Contemporary Medals, March 1910.* Edited by Agnes Baldwin. Rev. ed. New York, 1911.

Indian Peace Medals: Belden, Bauman L. *Indian Peace Medals Issued in the United States 1789-1889.* New York, 1927; reprint ed., New Milford, Connecticut, 1966.

Jones: Jones, Mark. *The Art of the Medal.* London, 1979.

Julian: Julian, R.W. *Medals of the United States Mint: The First Century, 1792-1892.* El Cajon, California, 1977.

King: King, Robert P. "Lincoln in Numismatics." *The Numismatist* 37 (1921), pp. 53-171.

Lami: Lami, Stanislas. *Dictionnaire des sculpteurs de L'école française au dix-neuvième siècle.* 4 vols. Paris, 1914-1921.

Loubat: Loubat, J. F. *The Medallic History of the United States of America, 1776-1876.* New York, 1880.

MacNeil 1977: MacNeil, Neil. *The President's Medal, 1789-1977.* New York, 1977.

Marx 1897: Marx, Roger. *Les médailleurs français depuis 1789.* Paris, 1897.

Marx 1898: Marx, Roger. *Les médailleurs français contemporains.* Paris, 1898.

Marx 1901: Marx, Roger. *Les médailleurs modernes à l'Exposition Universelle de 1900.* Paris, 1901.

MFA 1986: Greenthal, Kathryn; Kozol, Paula M.; and Ramirez, Jan Seidler. *American Figurative Sculpture in the Museum of Fine Arts, Boston.* Boston, 1986.

NSS 1923: National Sculpture Society. *Exhibition of American Sculpture Catalogue.* New York, 1923.

Romantics to Rodin: Fusco, Peter, and Janson, H. W., eds. *The Romantics to Rodin: French 19th-Century Sculpture from North American Collections.* Los Angeles, 1980.

Rulau and Fuld: Rulau, Russell and Fuld, George. *Medallic Portraits of Washington.* Iola, Wisconsin, 1985.

Stahl: Stahl, Alan M. "The American Industrial Medal." *The Numismatist* 97 (1984), pp. 2066-73.

Taft: Taft, Lorado. *The History of American Sculpture.* New York, 1903; rev. ed., 1930.

U.S. Mint 1972: Failor, Kenneth M. and Hayden, Eleonora. *Medals of the United States Mint.* Washington, DC, 1972.

Vermeule: Vermeule, Cornelius. *Numismatic Art in America: Aesthetics of the United States Coinage.* Cambridge, Massachusetts, 1971.

Whitney 1976: Whitney Museum of American Art. *200 Years of American Sculpture.* New York, 1976.

Index by Artist

Index of Illustrated Medals